THE ULTIMATE BLACKSTONE OUTDOOR GAS GRIDDLE COOKBOOK

2000 Days of Simple and Delicious Recipes, Secret Tips, and Grilling Master Techniques for Beginners to Cook Like a Pro.

By Julieta Paul

Copyright © 2024 by Julieta Paul

All rights reserved. No part of this book may be reproduced, distributed, or transmitted in any form or by any means, including photocopying, recording, or other electronic or mechanical methods, without the prior written permission of the author, except for brief quotations embodied in critical reviews and specific other noncommercial uses permitted by copyright law.

Disclaimer

This cookbook is for educational purposes only and does not provide health or nutritional advice. The author is not a professional chef or nutritionist but has spent years perfecting these recipes. While efforts have been made to ensure accuracy, the author assumes no responsibility for errors or inconsistencies.

Food preparation carries inherent risks, including foodborne illness. Readers should follow all safety precautions and guidelines provided by food safety authorities. The author is not liable for any adverse outcomes from using the information or recipes in this cookbook.

Using this cookbook, you agree to indemnify and hold the author harmless from any claims or liabilities arising from its use.
First Edition, 2024

Conclusion

Thank you for joining me on this culinary journey with The Ultimate Blackstone Outdoor Gas Griddle Cookbook. From selecting the finest cuts of meat to mastering advanced cooking techniques, you now have the tools and knowledge to create delicious, restaurant-quality meals right in your backyard. Whether you're cooking for family and friends or simply indulging in your passion for grilling, this cookbook is designed to help you achieve perfection on your Blackstone griddle. Remember, the key to great cooking is practice, experimentation, and a love for the craft. Happy grilling!

TABLE OF CONTENTS

Introduction 5

Get Your Free Exclusive Bonuses Now 6

Chapter 1: Getting Started with the Blackstone Griddle 7

Chapter 2: Blackstone Grill Advanced Cooking Techniques 12

Chapter 3: Meat Preparation and Cooking Advice 15

Chapter 4: Recipes 21

Breakfast 21
   1. Spinach and Feta Breakfast Wraps 21
   2. Banana Nut Pancakes with Honey Butter 21
   3. Classic Eggs Benedict with Hollandaise Sauce .. 22
   4. Hearty Breakfast Hash with Sausage and Peppers 22
   5. Berry Compote French Toast 23
   6. Cheesy Ham and Veggie Omelette 23

Poultry 24
   7. Crispy Honey Mustard Chicken Tenders 24
   8. Lemon Garlic Grilled Chicken Breasts 24
   9. Spicy BBQ Chicken Thighs 25
   10. Teriyaki Chicken Skewers with Pineapple 25
   11. Herb Marinated Chicken Kabobs 26
   12. Creamy Pesto Chicken Breasts 26
   13. Mediterranean Grilled Chicken Salad 27

Beef 27
   14. Classic Beef Tacos with Fresh Salsa 27
   15. Beef and Vegetable Stir-Fry 28
   16. Cheesy Beef and Bean Quesadillas 28
   17. Beef Stroganoff with Creamy Mushrooms 29
   18. Tex-Mex Beef Nachos with Jalapeños 29
   19. Southwestern Beef Enchiladas 30

Lamb 30
   20. Lamb Meatballs with Mint Yogurt Sauce 30
   21. Greek Lamb Gyros with Tzatziki 31
   22. Lamb and Potato Skillet 31
   23. Lamb Souvlaki with Lemon Rice 32
   24. Curried Lamb Skewers with Coconut Rice 32
   25. Lamb Pita Pockets with Hummus 33

Pork 33
   26. BBQ Pulled Pork Sandwiches 33
   27. Sweet and Sour Pork Skewers 34
   28. Pork and Pineapple Fried Rice 34
   29. Crispy Pork Carnitas Tacos 35

   30. Honey Garlic Pork Loin Medallions 35
   31. Pork Fajitas with Bell Peppers 36
Sauce 36
   32. Smoky Chipotle BBQ Sauce 36
   33. Creamy Garlic Herb Aioli 37
   34. Classic Marinara with Fresh Basil 37
   35. Spicy Sriracha Mayo 38
   36. Zesty Lemon Dill Sauce 38
   37. Savory Mushroom Gravy 39

Vegetables and Side Dishes 39
   38. Grilled Asparagus with Parmesan and Lemon ... 39
   39. Honey-Glazed Carrots with Thyme 40
   40. Sautéed Brussels Sprouts with Bacon 40
   41. Charred Corn and Black Bean Salad 41
   42. Garlic Butter Green Beans 41
   43. Spicy Roasted Cauliflower 42
   44. Stuffed Portobello Mushrooms with Spinach and Feta 42
   45. Crispy Herb-Roasted Potatoes 43
   46. Loaded Baked Potato Skins 43
   47. Southwest Quinoa Salad 44

Burger Recipes 44
   48. Classic All-American Cheeseburger 44
   49. Smoky BBQ Bacon Burger 45
   50. Spicy Jalapeño Pepper Jack Burger 45
   51. Mushroom Swiss Burger with Caramelized Onions 46
   52. Avocado Bacon Ranch Burger 46
   53. Blue Cheese and Caramelized Onion Burger ... 47
   54. Hawaiian Teriyaki Pineapple Burger 47
   55. Tex-Mex Guacamole Burger 48
   56. Garlic Parmesan Turkey Burger 48
   57. Mediterranean Lamb Burger with Tzatziki 49
   58. Pesto Chicken Caprese Burger 49
   59. Chipotle Black Bean Veggie Burger 50
   60. Spicy Sriracha Salmon Burger 50
   61. Greek Feta and Spinach Burger 51
   62. Citrus Herb Grilled Salmon Burger 51

Hot Dog Recipes 52
   63. Classic New York Style Hot Dog 52
   64. Chicago-Style Loaded Hot Dog 52
   65. Bacon-Wrapped Jalapeño Cheese Dog 53
   66. Chili Cheese Dog with Onions 53
   67. BBQ Pulled Pork Hot Dog 54

Steak Recipes 54
   68. Garlic Butter Ribeye Steak 54
   69. Chimichurri Flank Steak 55
   70. Peppercorn Crusted Strip Steak 55
   71. Classic American Grilled Sirloin 56

72. Herb-Rubbed T-Bone Steak 56
73. Balsamic Glazed Filet Mignon 57
74. Southwest Spiced Hanger Steak 57
75. Coffee Rubbed Sirloin Steak 58
76. Blue Cheese Crusted New York Strip 58
77. Teriyaki Glazed Flat Iron Steak 59

Fish and Seafood Recipes 59
78. Lemon Garlic Grilled Shrimp 59
79. Honey Soy Glazed Salmon 60
80. Garlic Butter Scallops 60
81. Teriyaki Mahi-Mahi with Pineapple Salsa 61
82. Spicy Grilled Swordfish Steaks 61
83. Citrus Herb Grilled Tilapia 62
84. Dill and Lemon Salmon Fillets 62
85. Maple Mustard Glazed Salmon 63

Salad Recipes 63
86. Grilled Romaine Caesar Salad 63
87. Mediterranean Quinoa Salad with Feta and Olives 64
88. Strawberry Spinach Salad with Balsamic Vinaigrette 64
89. Avocado and Tomato Salad with Lime Dressing 65
90. Grilled Chicken Cobb Salad 65

Recipes for Special Occasions 66
91. Garlic Butter Lobster Tails 66
92. Herb-Crusted Rack of Lamb 66
93. Tropical Mango and Avocado Ceviche with Fish 67
94. Balsamic Glazed Duck Breast 67
95. Grilled Surf and Turf (Steak and Shrimp) 68
96. Maple Glazed Holiday Ham 68
97. Prosciutto-Wrapped Asparagus Bundles 69

Low Calories Recipes 69
98. Grilled Lemon Herb Chicken Breast 69
99. Zesty Shrimp and Veggie Skewers 70
100. Spicy Cauliflower Steaks 70
101. Turkey and Veggie Lettuce Wraps 71
102. Blackened Tilapia with Mango Salsa 71
103. Grilled Portobello Mushrooms with Balsamic Glaze 72

Mexican Cuisine Recipes 72
104. Beef and Cheese Quesadillas 72

105. Grilled Chicken Tacos with Fresh Pico de Gallo 73
106. Pork Carnitas Tostadas 73
107. Shrimp Fajitas with Bell Peppers and Onions 74
108. Vegetarian Black Bean and Corn Enchiladas . 74
109. Carne Asada Burritos 75

Italian Cousin recipes 75
110. Margherita Grilled Pizza 75
111. Garlic Shrimp Scampi 76
112. Pesto Chicken Panini 76
113. Caprese Salad with Balsamic Glaze 77
114. Sausage and Pepper Hoagies 77
115. Grilled Vegetable Antipasto 78
116. Lemon Herb Grilled Chicken Piccata 78

Asian Cuisine Recipes 79
117. Ginger Soy Chicken Stir-Fry 79
118. Beef and Broccoli Stir-Fry 79
119. Spicy Szechuan Shrimp 80
120. Teriyaki Chicken Bowls with Steamed Rice 80
121. Soy Glazed Salmon with Sesame 81
122. Sweet and Sour Pork Stir-Fry 81

Latin-American Recipes 82
123. Argentinian Grilled Chimichurri Steak 82
124. Peruvian Chicken with Aji Verde Sauce 82
125. Cuban Mojo Pork Tacos 83
126. Chilean Pebre Sauce with Grilled Bread 83
127. Brazilian Grilled Pineapple with Cinnamon 84

Desserts 84
128. Grilled Peaches with Honey and Mascarpone 84
129. Cinnamon Sugar Grilled Pineapple Rings 85
130. Griddled Pound Cake with Berries and Cream 85
131. S'mores Quesadillas 86

Snacks 86
132. Grilled Cheese Sandwiches with Tomato Soup Dip 86
133. Crispy Zucchini Fritters 87
134. Loaded Nachos with Griddled Beef 87
135. Cheesy Queso Dip with Griddled Jalapeños . 88
136. Sweet Potato Fries with Spicy Aioli 88

INTRODUCTION

Imagine yourself in your backyard at sunset, with the aroma of sizzling steak filling the air. You've always wanted to create that perfect, restaurant-quality meal at home, but something holds you back. Maybe it's a lack of experience, the overwhelming variety of recipes, technical challenges, or simply the time constraints of a busy life. These obstacles can make outdoor cooking seem daunting.

Welcome to The Ultimate Blackstone Outdoor Gas Griddle Cookbook. Whether you're a novice or a seasoned griller, this book is crafted to meet your needs. We understand the frustration of not knowing which cut of meat to choose, how to control the griddle's temperature, or how to find the right recipe that fits your schedule. Here, you'll find solutions to these problems and more.

With over two decades of culinary experience, I have faced and overcome the same challenges you do. My passion for grilling and professional expertise has culminated in this guide designed to empower you with the knowledge and skills needed to excel. Each recipe, tip, and technique in this book comes from years of hands-on experience and a genuine love for grilling.

As we embark on this culinary adventure together, you'll find that this book is more than just a collection of recipes. It's a roadmap to transforming your grilling skills and enhancing your outdoor cooking experience. Welcome to your ultimate guide to mastering your Blackstone griddle.

🎆 GET YOUR FREE EXCLUSIVE BONUSES NOW! 🎆

Download for Free – Simply Scan the QR Code Below!

Unlock the Full Potential of Your Blackstone Griddl
Get exclusive bonuses packed with expert tips, recipes, and tools to elevate your grilling—perfect for both beginners and seasoned pros!

BONUS 1: New Recipes Every Month!
Stay inspired with delicious new dishes delivered straight to your inbox each month. Enjoy creative and mouth-watering recipes that will keep your grilling fresh and exciting!

BONUS 2: Grill Maintenance Checklist for Blackstone Grill
Keep your Blackstone grill in top shape with this comprehensive maintenance checklist. Ensure your grill is always ready for perfect cooking results.

BONUS 3: 28-Day Meal Plan
Enjoy a complete, step-by-step meal plan to simplify your grilling. From breakfast to dinner, we've got every meal covered, making your griddle experience effortless.

BONUS 4: Shopping List
Spend less time planning and more time grilling! Our shopping list includes everything you need for the 28-day meal plan, ensuring you're prepared for a month of fantastic meals.

BONUS 5: Tips & Tricks
Master the art of grilling with professional tips & tricks designed to help you achieve the best results every time you cook.

SCAN THE QR CODE BELOW AND UNLOCK YOUR BONUSES NOW!

CHAPTER 1

Getting Started with the Blackstone Griddle

1. Benefits of Using a Blackstone Griddle

The Blackstone griddle offers several advantages for outdoor cooking. Its large, flat surface allows you to prepare multiple dishes simultaneously, making it ideal for gatherings or family meals. Its high heat capacity ensures perfect sears on meats and creates a delicious caramelized crust. The even heat distribution reduces hot spots, ensuring consistent cooking results.

The griddle's versatility lets you cook various foods, from breakfast staples like pancakes and bacon to dinner favorites like stir-fries and steaks. Its easy-to-clean surface and built-in grease management system simplify cleanup, letting you enjoy your meals more.

2. Types and Features of Blackstone Griddles

Choosing the right Blackstone griddle can significantly enhance your culinary experience. Blackstone offers various griddles, each designed for different cooking styles, spaces, and preferences. Here's a guide to the types of Blackstone griddles available:

Tabletop Griddles

Overview:
Compact and portable, perfect for convenience and portability.
It is ideal for camping trips, tailgating, picnics, small balconies, and limited outdoor spaces.

Features:
Single or dual burners for flexibility.
The cooking surface ranges from 17 to 22 inches and is suitable for small groups.
It uses small propane tanks for easy setup and use anywhere.

Popular Models:
Blackstone 17" Tabletop Griddle: Ideal for compact spaces and small gatherings.
Blackstone 22" Tabletop Griddle: A dual-burner option with more cooking surface.

Freestanding Griddles

Overview:
Larger and more versatile with built-in stands and shelves.
It is ideal for backyard grilling, outdoor kitchens, and larger gatherings.

Features:
Two to four burners for precise temperature control and multiple heat zones.
The cooking surface ranges from 28 to 36 inches, perfect for various foods.
Includes shelves and storage compartments for utensils and ingredients.

Popular Models:
Blackstone 28" Griddle Cooking Station: A two-burner model with ample space and storage.
Blackstone 36" Griddle Cooking Station: A four-burner model for larger groups.

Combo Griddles

Overview:
Combines a griddle with additional cooking surfaces, like a grill or range top.
It is ideal for home cooks who want multiple cooking methods.

Features:
Dual functionality with a griddle on one side and a grill or range top on the other.
Multiple burners for independent heat control.
Popular Models:
Blackstone Tailgater Combo: Combines a griddle and grill, perfect for outdoor events.
Blackstone Grill & Griddle Combo: Offers a large griddle surface and a separate grill section.

Electric Griddles

Overview:
Designed for convenient indoor cooking without the need for propane.
Ideal for apartment living and indoor kitchens.

Features:
Plug-and-play setup with a standard electrical outlet.
Provides consistent heat and uniform cooking.
Compact design suitable for countertops.

Popular Models:
Blackstone E-Series 17" Electric Tabletop Griddle: Compact and perfect for indoor cooking.
Blackstone E-Series 22" Electric Tabletop Griddle: Offers a larger surface with electric power.

3. Heat Zones
Creating and managing heat zones on your Blackstone griddle is critical to versatile and efficient cooking. By adjusting the heat of individual burners, you can establish different temperature zones across the griddle surface:

High Heat Zone: This zone is ideal for searing meats and achieving a crispy exterior. It is perfect for cooking steaks, burgers, and other items that benefit from a quick, high-temperature sear.
Medium Heat Zone: This is suitable for cooking vegetables, pancakes, eggs, and other foods that require moderate, consistent temperature. It allows for even cooking without burning.
Low Heat Zone: This is great for keeping food warm, cooking delicate items like fish, and simmering sauces. It provides gentle, consistent heat to avoid overcooking.
Utilizing these heat zones allows you to cook various dishes simultaneously, ensuring each one is perfectly prepared.

4. Low, Medium, and High Heat: Definitions and Common Uses

Understanding the different heat levels on your Blackstone griddle is essential for practical cooking:
Low Heat (200-300°F): This gentle heat is perfect for simmering sauces, cooking delicate foods like fish, and keeping food warm. It allows for slow, controlled cooking without burning.
Medium Heat (300-375°F): This versatile temperature range is suitable for cooking most foods, including vegetables, eggs, pancakes, and proteins like chicken and pork. It provides a good balance between cooking speed and control.
High Heat (375-450°F): High heat is ideal for searing meats, stir-frying, and achieving a crispy crust on foods. This temperature quickly caramelizes the exterior of meats, locking in juices and flavor.

5. Using a Thermometer

Using a thermometer ensures your food is cooked to the correct temperature for safety and taste:
Instant-Read Thermometers: These provide quick, accurate readings perfect for checking steaks, burgers, and other meats.
Probe Thermometers: These continuously monitor the internal temperature of more significant cuts. Insert the probe into the thickest part of the meat, and the connected display shows the current temperature, helping you avoid undercooking or overcooking.

6. Heat Adjustment

Proper heat adjustment is key for optimal cooking on your Blackstone griddle:
Control Knobs: Use these to increase or decrease heat output. Familiarize yourself with these controls for precise temperature adjustments.
Creating Heat Zones: Adjust burners to different levels to create distinct heat zones. This allows you to cook various foods at their ideal temperatures simultaneously.

7. Essential Tools and Accessories

Maximize your Blackstone griddle experience with the right tools and accessories. Here's a guide to essential items and recommendations to enhance your outdoor cooking setup:

Spatulas
Wide, Flat Spatulas: Ideal for flipping and moving food. Opt for sturdy, heat-resistant stainless steel with beveled edges.
Perforated Spatulas: Allow grease and juices to drain, perfect for burgers and steaks.

Tongs
Locking Tongs: Great for turning and lifting without piercing. Choose tongs with silicone tips for a secure grip and to prevent scratching.

Griddle Press
Even Cooking: This method applies uniform pressure for even cooking and browning. Heavy-duty, heat-resistant presses, preferably cast iron, are best.

Oil Squeeze Bottles
Controlled Application: Essential for even oil application. Look for fine nozzles for better control.

Basting Covers
Melting Cheese and Steaming: Trap heat and steam for melting cheese or steaming vegetables. Stainless steel covers with heat-resistant handles are ideal.

Scrapers and Cleaning Tools
Griddle Scrapers: Essential for cleaning. Choose scrapers with replaceable blades.
Grill Brushes: Maintain the surface by removing stuck-on food. Opt for strong bristles.

Cutting Boards
Durable and Hygienic: Essential for prepping ingredients. Use wooden or high-quality plastic boards that are easy to clean.

Storage Solutions
Tool Caddies and Organizers: Keep tools organized and within reach. Consider magnetic tool holders or hooks.

Seasoning and Marinade Brushes
Even Application: Essential for applying marinades, sauces, and seasonings. Choose heat-resistant silicone brushes that are easy to clean.

8. Tips for Maintaining and Cleaning the Griddle
Proper maintenance and cleaning of your Blackstone griddle ensure its longevity, performance, and safety. Here's how to keep your griddle in top condition:

Seasoning Your Griddle:
Why Seasoning is Important:
Creates a non-stick surface.
Prevents rust and corrosion.
Adds depth of flavor.

How to Season Your Griddle:
Clean: Wash with soap and water. Rinse and dry.
Apply Oil: Use high-heat oil (flaxseed, canola, or vegetable). Apply a thin, even layer.
Heat: Turn burners to high. Let the oil smoke for 15-20 minutes.
Repeat: Cool slightly, apply another oil layer, and repeat 3-4 times.

Daily Cleaning Routine
After Each Use:
Cool Down: Let the griddle cool slightly.
Scrape: Use a griddle scraper to remove debris and grease.
Wipe Down: Clean with a paper towel or soft cloth.

Apply Oil: Add a thin layer to maintain seasoning and prevent rust.

For Stubborn Residue
Water and Steam: Pour water on the warm griddle to create steam. Scrape to loosen bits.
Griddle Stone: Use for tough residue without damaging the seasoning.

Deep Cleaning Routine
Periodic Deep Cleaning:
Remove Burners: Follow the manufacturer's instructions.
Soap and Water: Use mild dish soap with warm water. Scrub with a sponge or brush.
Rinse Thoroughly: Ensure no soap residue remains.
Dry Completely: Use a cloth or paper towel to prevent rust.
Re-Season: Follow seasoning steps after deep cleaning.

Preventive Maintenance Tips
Cover When Not in Use: Use a heavy-duty cover to protect from the elements.
Store Indoors: Store indoors during harsh weather to prevent rust and damage.
Check for Rust: Regularly inspect and scrub any rust with steel wool, clean, and re-season.
Maintaining your Blackstone griddle properly ensures it performs well and lasts longer.

9. Safety Tips

Handling and Cleaning:
Heat Protection: Always use heat-resistant gloves when handling a hot griddle or performing maintenance tasks.
Proper Ventilation: Ensure your cooking area is well-ventilated, especially when using cleaning agents or creating steam during cleaning.
Avoid Abrasives: When cleaning, avoid using harsh abrasives that can damage the griddle surface or its seasoning.

CHAPTER 2

Blackstone Grill Advanced Cooking Techniques

Mastering your Blackstone grill involves advanced techniques that elevate your cooking and impress your guests. Here are expert tips to help you make the most of your Blackstone grill.

Searing for Perfect Crust
Technique:
Preheat to 450°F.
Lightly oil the surface.
Ensure meat is dry; press with a spatula for 2-3 minutes, then flip.

Benefits:
Locks in juices and creates a flavorful crust.

Using a Dome Lid for Steam Cooking
Technique:
Preheat the dome lid.
Add liquid around the food and cover immediately.

Benefits:
Retains moisture, cooks evenly, and enhances flavors.

Creating Multi-Zone Cooking Areas
Technique:
Adjust burners for high, medium, and low heat zones.
Move food between zones as needed.

Benefits:
Manages different cooking times and temperatures.

Basting for Enhanced Flavor
Technique:
Use a heat-resistant brush to apply marinades or butter.
Baste frequently while cooking.

Benefits:
Adds layers of flavor and keeps meats juicy.

Flash Cooking Vegetables
Technique:
Preheat to high heat, lightly oil and season vegetables, spread evenly, and toss frequently.

Benefits:
Retains color, texture, and nutrients.

Infusing Smoke Flavor
Technique:
Use a smoker box with wood chips, cook meat on low heat, cover with a dome lid.

Benefits:
Adds depth and complexity to dishes.

Griddle Breakfast Techniques
Technique:
Pancakes: Medium heat, use a squeeze bottle.
Eggs: Medium-low heat.
Bacon: Start on a cold griddle and turn to medium heat.

Benefits:
Perfect pancakes, fluffy eggs, and crispy bacon.

Caramelizing Onions and Vegetables
Technique:
Preheat to low heat; add oil and butter, and cook slowly.

Benefits:
Enhances sweetness and flavor.

Utilizing Griddle Presses
Technique:
Preheat the press and apply even pressure to the food.

Benefits:
Ensures even cooking and reduces time.

Rotating and Flipping Techniques
Technique:
Quarter turns for grill marks, flip once, use multiple spatulas for large items.

Benefits:
Evenly cooked, beautifully marked, and intact food.

Searing and Sautéing
Searing:
High heat, dry food, flip once.
Benefits: Enhances flavor and locks in juices.

Sautéing:
Medium heat, small pieces, toss frequently.
Benefits: Preserve texture and flavor.

Direct and Indirect Cooking
Direct Cooking:
High heat for quick searing.

Benefits:
Quick sear and crispy texture.

Indirect Cooking:
Low to medium heat, away from direct heat, cover.
Benefits: Even cooking for more significant cuts without burning.

CHAPTER 3

Meat Preparation and Cooking Advice

Cooking meat perfectly on your Blackstone griddle involves more than just heat. This chapter covers selecting the best cuts and cooking techniques for delicious and safe results.

Selecting Quality Meat

Beef
Ribeye: Rich marbling, tender, ideal for high-heat searing and grilling.
Tenderloin (Filet Mignon): Lean, tender, subtle flavor, best cooked to medium-rare.
Sirloin: Versatile and flavorful, suitable for grilling, searing, or broiling.
Brisket: Tougher cut that becomes tender when slow-cooked, perfect for smoking or braising.

Pork
Pork Chops: Bone-in or boneless, great for grilling or searing. Bone-in chops are juicier.
Pork Tenderloin: Lean, tender, cooks quickly, perfect for grilling or roasting.
Pork Shoulder (Boston Butt): Ideal for slow-cooking methods, well-marbled and flavorful.

Lamb
Lamb Chops: Tender and flavorful, ideal for grilling or pan-searing.
Leg of Lamb: Versatile, can be roasted, grilled, or braised, often marinated for flavor.
Lamb Shank: Best for slow-cooking methods like braising.

Chicken
Chicken Breasts: Lean, versatile, great for grilling, baking, and sautéing.
Chicken Thighs: Juicier and more flavorful than breasts, suitable for various cooking methods.
Whole Chicken: Versatile for roasting, grilling, or slow cooking, economical for multiple meals.

Choosing Freshness: Tips for Selecting the Freshest Meats

	Color	Texture	Smell
Beef	Bright red with marbling. Avoid brown or gray.	Firm, not slimy or sticky.	Mild and clean. Avoid off or sour smells.
Pork	Pinkish-red with white fat. Avoid dull gray.	Firm and moist, not dry or slimy.	Neutral, slightly sweet. Avoid strong, sour odors.
Lamb	Light to dark red. Fat should be firm and white, not yellow.	Firm and elastic.	Mild, slightly gamey. Avoid strong, unpleasant odors.
Chicken	Pinkish hue. Avoid gray or yellow.	Firm and moist. Avoid slimy or sticky.	Neutral. Avoid sour or off odors.

Prepping Meat for Cooking

Thawing Techniques:
Refrigerator Thawing: This is the safest method, allowing even thawing. Place meat in a dish to catch juices.
Cold Water Thawing: Submerge in cold water, changing every 30 minutes. Ensure the meat is sealed in a plastic bag.
Microwave Thawing: Use if short on time, but cook immediately after thawing to prevent bacteria growth.

Marinating Methods:
Basic Marinade: Combine oil, acid (vinegar or citrus), and seasonings. Marinate in the fridge for at least 30 minutes, ideally overnight.
Vacuum Marinating: A vacuum sealer expedites marinating, allowing deeper flavor penetration.
Injecting Marinade: Use a marinade injector for larger cuts.

Seasoning Tips:
Salt and Pepper: Classic combination to enhance natural flavors.
Herbs and Spices: Try rosemary and garlic for lamb or cumin and chili powder for beef.
Dry Rubs: Mix spices and herbs into a paste and rub onto meat for a flavorful crust.

Temperature and Timing

Cooking Temperatures: Recommended Internal Temperatures for Different Meats

Proper cooking temperatures ensure your meat is safe to eat and cooked to the desired doneness. The best way to measure internal temperatures accurately is to use a meat thermometer.

	Rare	Medium-Rare	Medium	Medium-Well	Well-Done
Beef	120-125°F (Cool red center)	130-135°F (Warm red center)	135-145°F (Warm pink center)	145-155°F (Slightly pink center)	155°F and above (Little or no pink)
Pork		145°F (Juicy and slightly pink)	150°F (Less pink, still juicy)		160°F and above (Fully cooked, less juicy)
Lamb	125°F (Cool red center)	130-135°F (Warm red center)	135-145°F (Warm pink center)		155°F and above (Little or no pink)
Chicken and Turkey	**White Meat** 165°F (Juicy and fully cooked)		**Dark Meat** 175°F (Tender and fully cooked)		
Fish	**General:** 145°F (Opaque and flakes easily with a fork)				

Resting Meat: Why and How Long to Let Meat Rest Before Serving

Why Rest Meat:
Juice Redistribution: During cooking, juices move toward the surface of the meat. Resting allows these juices to redistribute throughout the meat, producing a juicier final product.
Ease of Slicing: Rested meat is firmer and easier to slice without losing moisture.

How Long to Rest Meat:
Steaks and Chops: 5-10 minutes.
Larger Cuts (Roasts, Whole Chicken): 15-30 minutes.
Small Cuts (Burgers, Chicken Breasts): 3-5 minutes.

Resting Tips:
Cover Loosely: Tent the meat with foil to keep it warm while resting without trapping steam, which can make the crust soggy.

Cooking Duration: General Guidelines for Cooking Times Based on Thickness and Type of Meat

		Rare	Medium-Rare	Medium	Well-Done
Beef	**Steaks (1 inch thick)**	4-5 minutes total (2-2.5 minutes per side)	6-7 minutes total (3-3.5 minutes per side)	7-8 minutes total (3.5-4 minutes per side)	10-12 minutes total (5-6 minutes per side)
	Burgers (1/2 inch thick)		6-7 minutes total (3-3.5 minutes per side)	8-9 minutes total (4-4.5 minutes per side)	10-12 minutes total (5-6 minutes per side)
Pork	**Pork Chops (1 inch thick)**		6-7 minutes total (3-3.5 minutes per side)	8-9 minutes total (4-4.5 minutes per side)	10-12 minutes total (5-6 minutes per side)
	Pork Tenderloin		20-25 minutes total (whole tenderloin)	25-30 minutes total (whole tenderloin)	30-35 minutes total (whole tenderloin)
Lamb	**Lamb Chops (1 inch thick)**	4-5 minutes total (2-2.5 minutes per side)	6-7 minutes total (3-3.5 minutes per side)	7-8 minutes total (3.5-4 minutes per side)	10-12 minutes total (5-6 minutes per side)
	Leg of Lamb		1.5-2 hours total (whole leg, indirect heat)	2-2.5 hours total (whole leg, indirect heat)	2.5-3 hours total (whole leg, indirect heat)

		Medium	Well-Done
Chicken	Breasts (Boneless, 1 inch thick)	8-10 minutes total (4-5 minutes per side)	10-12 minutes total (5-6 minutes per side)
	Thighs (Bone-In)	20-25 minutes total (10-12.5 minutes per side)	25-30 minutes total (12.5-15 minutes per side)
	Whole Chicken	8-9 minutes total (4-4.5 minutes per side)	1.5-2 hours total (indirect heat)
Fish	Fillets (1 inch thick)	8-10 minutes total (4-5 minutes per side)	10-12 minutes total (5-6 minutes per side)
	Whole Fish	20-25 minutes total (whole fish, indirect heat)	25-30 minutes total (whole fish, indirect heat)

Timing Tips

Thickness Matters: Adjust cooking times based on the thickness of the meat. Thicker cuts require longer cooking times.
Monitor Closely: Use a meat thermometer to check for doneness and avoid overcooking.
Adjust for Preference: These guidelines are for medium doneness. Adjust cooking times slightly if you prefer your meat to be more or less done.

Meat Safety Tips

Avoiding Cross-Contamination:

Separate Cutting Boards: Use different boards for raw meat and other foods.
Clean Utensils: Wash knives and utensils thoroughly after contact with raw meat.
Hand Washing: Always wash hands with soap and water after handling raw meat.

Safe Handling and Storage:

Refrigeration: Store meat at 32-40°F. Use ground meats within 1-2 days and whole cuts within 3-5 days.
Freezing: Wrap the meat tightly in plastic wrap, foil, or vacuum seal. Label with the date. Store at 0°F or lower.

Recognizing Spoilage:

Color Change: Brown or gray discoloration can indicate spoilage.
Odor: A sour or off smell is a clear sign of spoilage.
Texture: A slimy or sticky texture means the meat is no longer safe to eat.

Troubleshooting Common Issues

Overcooking:
Prevention: Use a meat thermometer. Cook to slightly below the desired temperature; meat continues to cook while resting.
Fixes: Slice thinly and serve with a flavorful sauce.

Dry Meat Solutions:
Brining: Soak in a saltwater solution before cooking.
Basting: Regularly baste with juices or marinade.
Sauces: Serve with a rich sauce or gravy.

CHAPTER 4: RECIPES

BREAKFAST

1. Spinach and Feta Breakfast Wraps

- Difficulty Level: Easy
- Prep Time: 10 minutes
- Cooking Time: 10 minutes
- Total Time: 20 minutes
- Temperature: Medium Heat
- Cooking Type: Griddling
- Servings: 1 person

Ingredients:
- 1 whole wheat tortilla
- 1 cup fresh spinach, chopped
- 1/4 cup crumbled feta cheese
- 2 large eggs
- 1 tbsp olive oil
- Salt and pepper to taste

Nutritional value (per serving):
Calories: 300 | Protein: 14g | Carbohydrates: 28g | Fats: 14g | Fiber: 4g

Instructions:
1. Preheat the Griddle: Set your gas griddle to medium heat and let it warm.
2. Cook the Spinach: Drizzle 1/2 tbsp of olive oil on the griddle. Add the chopped spinach and sauté until wilted, about 2-3 minutes. Set aside.
3. Cook the Eggs: Drizzle the remaining 1/2 tbsp of olive oil on the griddle. Crack the eggs onto the griddle, season with salt and pepper, and scramble until fully cooked, about 3-4 minutes.
4. Assemble the Wrap: Place the tortilla on the griddle for 30 seconds to warm it up. Remove from heat, and layer the spinach, scrambled eggs, and feta cheese in the center of the tortilla.
5. Wrap It Up: Fold the sides of the tortilla over the filling, then roll it up tightly.
6. Final Toast: Place the wrap back on the griddle, seam side down, and toast for 1-2 minutes on each side until golden and crispy.

Serving Suggestions:
1. Serve with a side of fresh fruit or a small mixed greens salad.

2. Banana Nut Pancakes with Honey Butter

- Difficulty Level: Easy
- Prep Time: 10 minutes
- Cooking Time: 15 minutes
- Total Time: 25 minutes
- Temperature: Medium Heat
- Cooking Type: Griddling
- Servings: 1 person

Ingredients:
- 1/2 cup whole wheat flour
- 1/2 tsp baking powder
- 1/4 tsp baking soda
- 1/4 tsp salt
- 1/2 cup buttermilk
- 1 ripe banana, mashed
- 1 tbsp honey
- 1/4 cup chopped walnuts
- 1 tbsp butter (for cooking)
- 1 tbsp honey butter (for serving)

Nutritional value (per serving):
Calories: 450 | Protein: 10g | Carbohydrates: 60g | Fats: 18g | Fiber: 5g

Instructions:
1. Preheat the Griddle: Set your gas griddle to medium heat.
2. Prepare the Batter: In a mixing bowl, combine flour, baking powder, baking soda, and salt. In another bowl, mix buttermilk, mashed banana, and honey. Combine wet and dry ingredients, then fold in chopped walnuts.
3. Cook the Pancakes: Melt 1 tbsp of butter on the griddle. Pour 1/4 cup of batter per pancake onto the griddle. Cook for 2-3 minutes until bubbles form on the surface, then flip and cook for another 2-3 minutes until golden brown.
4. Serve: Top with a dollop of honey butter.

Serving Suggestions:
1. Serve with additional banana slices and a drizzle of maple syrup.

3. Classic Eggs Benedict with Hollandaise Sauce

Difficulty Level: Medium | *Prep Time:* 15 minutes | *Cooking Time:* 15 minutes
Total Time: 30 minutes | *Temperature:* Medium Heat | *Cooking Type:* Griddling, Sautéing | *Servings:* 1 person

Ingredients:
- 1 English muffin, split and toasted
- 2 large eggs
- 2 slices Canadian bacon
- 1 tbsp butter
- 1 tbsp white vinegar

For Hollandaise Sauce:
- 2 egg yolks
- 1/4 cup melted butter
- 1 tbsp lemon juice
- Salt and pepper to taste

Nutritional value (per serving):
Calories: 500 | Protein: 20g
Carbohydrates: 28g | Fats: 36g | Fiber: 2g

Instructions:
1. **Preheat the Griddle:** Set your gas griddle to medium heat.
2. **Cook the Canadian Bacon:** Melt 1 tbsp butter on the griddle. Cook the Canadian bacon until browned on both sides, about 2-3 minutes per side. Set aside.
3. **Poach the Eggs:** Bring a small pot of water to a simmer and add white vinegar. Create a gentle whirlpool in the water and crack eggs into the center. Poach for 3-4 minutes until the whites are set.
4. **Prepare the Hollandaise Sauce:** Whisk egg yolks and lemon juice in a heatproof bowl over simmering water. Slowly add melted butter while whisking continuously until the sauce thickens. Season with salt and pepper.
5. **Assemble:** Place toasted English muffin halves on a plate, top each with a slice of Canadian bacon and a poached egg, and drizzle with hollandaise sauce.
6. **Serving Suggestions:**
7. Garnish with chopped chives and serve with a side of fresh fruit.

4. Hearty Breakfast Hash with Sausage and Peppers

Difficulty Level: Medium | *Prep Time:* 10 minutes | *Cooking Time:* 20 minutes
Total Time: 30 minutes | *Temperature:* Medium-High Heat | *Cooking Type:* Griddling, Sautéing | *Servings:* 1 person

Ingredients:
- 2 medium potatoes, diced
- 1/2 bell pepper, diced
- 1/2 onion, diced
- 2 breakfast sausage links, sliced
- 2 tbsp olive oil
- Salt and pepper to taste

Nutritional value (per serving):
Calories: 450 | Protein: 20g
Carbohydrates: 35g | Fats: 25g | Fiber: 5g

Instructions:
1. **Preheat the Griddle:** Set your gas griddle to medium-high heat.
2. **Cook the Potatoes:** Drizzle 1 tbsp of olive oil on the griddle. Add diced potatoes and cook, stirring occasionally, until browned and crispy, about 10 minutes.
3. **Add Vegetables and Sausage:** Drizzle the remaining olive oil and add bell pepper, onion, and sausage. Cook until the vegetables are tender and the sausage is browned, about 7-8 minutes.
4. **Season:** Season with salt and pepper to taste and cook for 2 minutes to blend flavors.

Serving Suggestions:
1. Serve with a fried egg on top and a side of toast.

5. Berry Compote French Toast

Difficulty Level: Easy | Prep Time: 10 minutes | Cooking Time: 15 minutes
Total Time: 25 minutes | Temperature: Medium Heat | Cooking Type: Griddling | Servings: 1 person

Ingredients:
- 2 slices of bread (preferably day-old)
- 1/2 cup milk
- 1 large egg
- 1 tsp vanilla extract
- 1/2 tsp cinnamon
- 1 tbsp butter
- For Berry Compote:
- 1/2 cup mixed berries (fresh or frozen)
- 1 tbsp honey
- 1 tsp lemon juice

Instructions:
1. Preheat the Griddle: Set your gas griddle to medium heat.
2. Prepare the Batter: In a bowl, whisk together milk, egg, vanilla extract, and cinnamon.
3. Cook the French Toast: Dip each slice of bread into the batter, ensuring both sides are well-coated. Melt butter on the griddle and cook the bread slices until golden brown, about 3-4 minutes per side.
4. Make the Berry Compote: Combine the berries, honey, and lemon juice in a small saucepan over medium heat. Cook until the berries are softened and the mixture is syrupy about 5-7 minutes.
5. Serve: Top the French toast with berry compote.

Nutritional value (per serving):
Calories: 400 | Protein: 12g | Carbohydrates: 60g | Fats: 12g | Fiber: 6g

Serving Suggestions:
1. Dust with powdered sugar and serve with a side of yogurt.

6. Cheesy Ham and Veggie Omelette

Difficulty Level: Easy | Prep Time: 10 minutes | Cooking Time: 10 minutes
Total Time: 20 minutes | Temperature: Medium Heat | Cooking Type: Griddling, Sautéing | Servings: 1 person

Ingredients:
- 2 large eggs
- 1/4 cup diced ham
- 1/4 cup shredded cheddar cheese
- 1/4 cup diced bell pepper
- 1/4 cup diced onion
- 1 tbsp butter
- Salt and pepper to taste

Instructions:
1. Preheat the Griddle: Set your gas griddle to medium heat.
2. Sauté the Vegetables: Melt 1/2 tbsp butter on the griddle. Add diced bell pepper, onion and sauté until tender, about 3-4 minutes. Remove from heat and set aside.
3. Prepare the Eggs: Whisk the eggs with a pinch of salt and pepper in a bowl.
4. Cook the Omelette: Melt the remaining butter on the griddle. Pour the beaten eggs onto the griddle and let them cook for 2-3 minutes until they start to set.
5. Add Fillings: Evenly distribute the sautéed vegetables, diced ham, and shredded cheese over one-half of the omelette.
6. Fold the Omelette: Carefully fold the other half over the fillings using a spatula. Cook for 2 minutes until the cheese is melted and the omelette is fully cooked.

Nutritional value (per serving):
Calories: 350 | Protein: 20g | Carbohydrates: 8g | Fats: 26g | Fiber: 2g

Serving Suggestions:
1. Serve with a side of toast and fresh fruit.

POULTRY

7. Crispy Honey Mustard Chicken Tenders

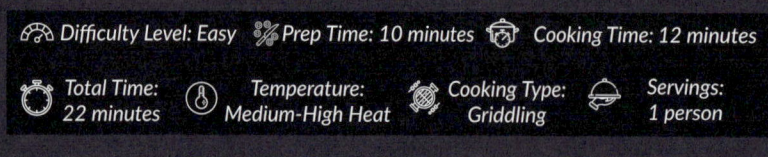

Difficulty Level: Easy | Prep Time: 10 minutes | Cooking Time: 12 minutes
Total Time: 22 minutes | Temperature: Medium-High Heat | Cooking Type: Griddling | Servings: 1 person

Ingredients:
- 1 chicken breast, cut into tenders
- 1/4 cup honey
- 1/4 cup Dijon mustard
- 1/2 cup panko breadcrumbs
- 1/4 cup all-purpose flour
- 1 large egg, beaten
- 1 tbsp olive oil
- Salt and pepper to taste

Instructions:
1. Preheat the Griddle: Set your gas griddle to medium-high heat.
2. Prepare the Honey Mustard Mixture: Mix honey and Dijon mustard in a bowl until well combined.
3. Coat the Chicken: Season the chicken tenders with salt and pepper. Dredge each tender in flour, dip in the beaten egg, and coat with panko breadcrumbs.
4. Cook the Tenders: Drizzle olive oil on the griddle. Place the chicken tenders on the griddle and cook for 6 minutes on each side or until golden brown and crispy.
5. Brush with Honey Mustard: During the last 2 minutes of cooking, brush the honey mustard mixture over the chicken tenders.

Serving Suggestions:
1. Serve with a side of mixed greens or sweet potato fries.

Nutritional value (per serving):
Calories: 350 | Protein: 25g | Carbohydrates: 30g | Fats: 15g | Fiber: 2g

8. Lemon Garlic Grilled Chicken Breasts

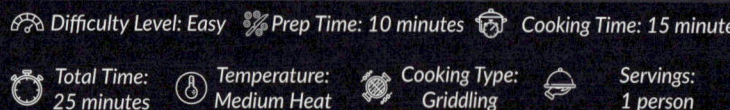

Difficulty Level: Easy | Prep Time: 10 minutes | Cooking Time: 15 minutes
Total Time: 25 minutes | Temperature: Medium Heat | Cooking Type: Griddling | Servings: 1 person

Ingredients:
- 1 chicken breast
- 2 tbsp olive oil
- 1 lemon, juiced
- 2 garlic cloves, minced
- 1 tsp dried oregano
- Salt and pepper to taste

Nutritional value (per serving):
Calories: 280 | Protein: 30g | Carbohydrates: 6g | Fats: 15g | Fiber: 1g

Instructions:
1. Preheat the Griddle: Set your gas griddle to medium heat.
2. Marinate the Chicken: In a bowl, combine olive oil, lemon juice, garlic, oregano, salt, and pepper. Marinate the chicken breast in this mixture for at least 30 minutes.
3. Cook the Chicken: Drizzle a bit of olive oil on the griddle. Place the chicken breast on the griddle and cook for 7-8 minutes per side or until the internal temperature reaches 165°F.
4. Serve: Let the chicken rest for a few minutes before slicing.

Serving Suggestions:
1. Serve with a side of grilled vegetables or a quinoa salad.

9. Spicy BBQ Chicken Thighs

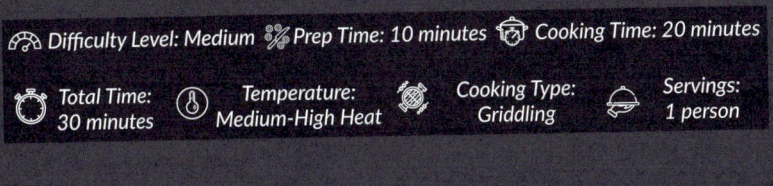

Difficulty Level: Medium | Prep Time: 10 minutes | Cooking Time: 20 minutes
Total Time: 30 minutes | Temperature: Medium-High Heat | Cooking Type: Griddling | Servings: 1 person

Ingredients:
- 2 chicken thighs
- 1/4 cup BBQ sauce
- 1 tbsp olive oil
- 1 tsp paprika
- 1/2 tsp cayenne pepper
- Salt and pepper to taste

Nutritional value (per serving):
Calories: 400 | Protein: 28g
Carbohydrates: 20g | Fats: 25g | Fiber: 2g

Instructions:
1. Preheat the Griddle: Set your gas griddle to medium-high heat.
2. Season the Chicken: Rub the chicken thighs with olive oil, paprika, cayenne pepper, salt, and pepper.
3. Cook the Chicken: Place the chicken thighs on the griddle and cook for 8-10 minutes per side, basting with BBQ sauce during the last 5 minutes of cooking.
4. Serve: Let the chicken rest for a few minutes before serving.

Serving Suggestions:
1. Serve with coleslaw or roasted potatoes.

10. Teriyaki Chicken Skewers with Pineapple

Difficulty Level: Medium | Prep Time: 15 minutes | Cooking Time: 10 minutes
Total Time: 25 minutes | Temperature: Medium-High Heat | Cooking Type: Griddling | Servings: 1 person

Ingredients:
- 1 chicken breast, cut into cubes
- 1/2 cup teriyaki sauce
- 1/2 cup pineapple chunks
- 1 bell pepper, cut into pieces
- 1 tbsp olive oil
- Salt and pepper to taste

Nutritional value (per serving):
Calories: 350 | Protein: 25g
Carbohydrates: 35g | Fats: 10g | Fiber: 3g

Instructions:
1. Preheat the Griddle: Set your gas griddle to medium-high heat.
2. Marinate the Chicken: Marinate the chicken cubes in teriyaki sauce for at least 30 minutes.
3. Assemble the Skewers: Thread the chicken, pineapple, and bell pepper onto skewers.
4. Cook the Skewers: Drizzle olive oil on the griddle. Place the skewers on the griddle and cook for 4-5 minutes per side, basting with extra teriyaki sauce.
5. Serve: Remove the skewers from the heat and serve immediately.

Serving Suggestions:
1. Serve with steamed rice or a side of Asian slaw.

11. Herb Marinated Chicken Kabobs

Difficulty Level: Medium | Prep Time: 15 minutes | Cooking Time: 15 minutes
Total Time: 30 minutes | Temperature: Medium-High Heat | Cooking Type: Griddling | Servings: 1 person

Ingredients:
- 1 chicken breast, cut into cubes
- 2 tbsp olive oil
- 1 tbsp lemon juice
- 1 tsp dried oregano
- 1 tsp dried thyme
- 1 garlic clove, minced
- 1 bell pepper, cut into pieces
- 1 small zucchini, cut into pieces
- Salt and pepper to taste

Nutritional value (per serving):
Calories: 300 | Protein: 28g | Carbohydrates: 10g | Fats: 15g | Fiber: 2g

Instructions:
1. Preheat the Griddle: Set your gas griddle to medium-high heat.
2. Marinate the Chicken: In a bowl, combine olive oil, lemon juice, oregano, thyme, garlic, salt, and pepper. Marinate the chicken cubes in this mixture for at least 30 minutes.
3. Assemble the Kabobs: Thread the chicken, bell pepper, and zucchini onto skewers.
4. Cook the Kabobs: Drizzle a bit of olive oil on the griddle. Place the kabobs on the griddle and cook for 5-6 minutes per side, rotating frequently.
5. Serve: Remove from heat and serve immediately.

Serving Suggestions:
1. Serve with a side of couscous or grilled vegetables.

12. Creamy Pesto Chicken Breasts

Difficulty Level: Easy | Prep Time: 10 minutes | Cooking Time: 15 minutes
Total Time: 25 minutes | Temperature: Medium Heat | Cooking Type: Griddling, Sautéing | Servings: 1 person

Ingredients:
- 1 chicken breast
- 2 tbsp pesto
- 1 tbsp olive oil
- 2 tbsp heavy cream
- Salt and pepper to taste

Nutritional value (per serving):
Calories: 320 | Protein: 30g | Carbohydrates: 6g | Fats: 20g | Fiber: 1g

Instructions:
1. Preheat the Griddle: Set your gas griddle to medium heat.
2. Season the Chicken: Rub the chicken breast with olive oil, salt, and pepper.
3. Cook the Chicken: Place the chicken breast on the griddle and cook for 7-8 minutes per side or until the internal temperature reaches 165°F.
4. Prepare the Pesto Sauce: Combine the pesto and heavy cream in a small saucepan. Heat over low heat until warm.
5. Serve: Top the cooked chicken breast with the creamy pesto sauce.

Serving Suggestions:
1. Serve with a side of roasted tomatoes or a mixed greens salad.

13. Mediterranean Grilled Chicken Salad

Difficulty Level: Easy	Prep Time: 15 minutes	Cooking Time: 10 minutes
Total Time: 25 minutes	Temperature: Medium Heat	Cooking Type: Griddling, Sautéing	Servings: 1 person

Ingredients:
- 1 chicken breast
- 2 tbsp olive oil
- 1 lemon, juiced
- 1 garlic clove, minced
- 1 tsp dried oregano
- Salt and pepper to taste
- 2 cups mixed greens
- 1/2 cucumber, sliced
- 1/2 cup cherry tomatoes, halved
- 1/4 cup Kalamata olives
- 1/4 cup crumbled feta cheese

Instructions:
1. Preheat the Griddle: Set your gas griddle to medium heat.
2. Marinate the Chicken: In a bowl, combine olive oil, lemon juice, garlic, oregano, salt, and pepper. Marinate the chicken breast in this mixture for at least 30 minutes.
3. Cook the Chicken: Place the chicken breast on the griddle and cook for 6-7 minutes per side or until the internal temperature reaches 165°F. Let it rest before slicing.
4. Assemble the Salad: In a large bowl, combine mixed greens, cucumber, cherry tomatoes, Kalamata olives, and feta cheese. Top with sliced chicken.
5. Serve: Drizzle with your favorite vinaigrette.

Serving Suggestions:
1. Serve with a side of pita bread and hummus.

Nutritional value (per serving):
Calories: 350 | Protein: 30g
Carbohydrates: 15g | Fats: 20g | Fiber: 5g

BEEF

14. Classic Beef Tacos with Fresh Salsa

Difficulty Level: Easy	Prep Time: 10 minutes	Cooking Time: 10 minutes
Total Time: 20 minutes	Temperature: Medium-High Heat	Cooking Type: Griddling, Sautéing	Servings: 1 person

Ingredients:
- 4 oz ground beef
- 1 tsp olive oil
- 1/2 tsp cumin
- 1/2 tsp chili powder
- Salt and pepper to taste
- 2 small flour or corn tortillas
- For Fresh Salsa:
- 1/2 cup diced tomatoes
- 1/4 cup diced onion
- 1/4 cup chopped cilantro
- 1 tbsp lime juice
- Salt to taste

Instructions:
1. Preheat the Griddle: Set your gas griddle to medium-high heat.
2. Cook the Beef: Drizzle olive oil on the griddle. Add the ground beef, cumin, chili powder, salt, and pepper. Cook for 5-7 minutes, breaking it up with a spatula until browned and cooked.
3. Prepare the Salsa: In a bowl, combine diced tomatoes, onion, cilantro, lime juice, and salt. Mix well.
4. Warm the Tortillas: Place the tortillas on the griddle for about 1 minute on each side to warm them.
5. Assemble the Tacos: Divide the cooked beef between the tortillas and top with fresh salsa.

Serving Suggestions:
1. Serve with a side of black beans or a small green salad.

Nutritional value (per serving):
Calories: 350 | Protein: 25g
Carbohydrates: 28g | Fats: 15g | Fiber: 5g

15. Beef and Vegetable Stir-Fry

Difficulty Level: Medium | Prep Time: 15 minutes | Cooking Time: 10 minutes
Total Time: 25 minutes | Temperature: Medium-High Heat | Cooking Type: Griddling, Sautéing | Servings: 1 person

Ingredients:

- 4 oz beef sirloin, thinly sliced
- 1 tbsp soy sauce
- 1 tsp sesame oil
- 1/2 bell pepper, sliced
- 1/2 cup broccoli florets
- 1/4 cup sliced carrots
- 1/4 cup sliced onions
- 1 garlic clove, minced
- 1 tbsp olive oil

Nutritional value *(per serving)*:

Calories: 400 | Protein: 30g
Carbohydrates: 20g | Fats: 20g | Fiber: 5g

Instructions:

1. Preheat the Griddle: Set your gas griddle to medium-high heat.
2. Marinate the Beef: Mix the beef with soy sauce and sesame oil in a bowl. Let it marinate for at least 10 minutes.
3. Cook the Vegetables: Drizzle olive oil on the griddle. Add bell pepper, broccoli, carrots, onions, and garlic. Cook for about 3-4 minutes, stirring frequently.
4. Cook the Beef: Push the vegetables to the side of the griddle. Add the marinated beef and cook for 2-3 minutes until browned and cooked.
5. Combine: Mix the beef and vegetables together on the griddle and cook for an additional 1-2 minutes.

Serving Suggestions:
1. Serve over steamed rice or noodles.

16. Cheesy Beef and Bean Quesadillas

Difficulty Level: Easy | Prep Time: 10 minutes | Cooking Time: 10 minutes
Total Time: 20 minutes | Temperature: Medium Heat | Cooking Type: Griddling | Servings: 1 person

Ingredients:

- 4 oz ground beef
- 1/4 cup canned black beans, drained and rinsed
- 1/2 cup shredded cheddar cheese
- 1/4 cup salsa
- 2 flour tortillas
- 1 tbsp olive oil
- Salt and pepper to taste

Nutritional value *(per serving)*:

Calories: 450 | Protein: 25g
Carbohydrates: 35g | Fats: 20g | Fiber: 7g

Instructions:

1. Preheat the Griddle: Set your gas griddle to medium heat.
2. Cook the Beef: Drizzle olive oil on the griddle. Add ground beef, salt, and pepper. Cook for about 5 minutes until browned. Add black beans and cook for an additional 2 minutes.
3. Assemble the Quesadilla: Place one tortilla on the griddle, sprinkle half of the cheese, then layer the beef and bean mixture. Top with the remaining cheese and the second tortilla.
4. Cook the Quesadilla: Cook for 2-3 minutes per side until the tortillas are golden brown and the cheese is melted.
5. Serve: Cut into wedges and serve with salsa.

Serving Suggestions:
1. Serve with a side of guacamole or sour cream.

17. Beef Stroganoff with Creamy Mushrooms

Difficulty Level: Medium | Prep Time: 10 minutes | Cooking Time: 15 minutes
Total Time: 25 minutes | Temperature: Medium-High Heat | Cooking Type: Griddling, Sautéing | Servings: 1 person

Ingredients:
- 4 oz beef sirloin, thinly sliced
- 1/2 cup sliced mushrooms
- 1/4 cup diced onions
- 1 garlic clove, minced
- 1/2 cup beef broth
- 1/4 cup sour cream
- 1 tbsp olive oil
- Salt and pepper to taste
- Cooked egg noodles (optional)

Instructions:
1. **Preheat the Griddle:** Set your gas griddle to medium-high heat.
2. **Cook the Beef:** Drizzle olive oil on the griddle. Add the beef slices, salt, and pepper. Cook for about 5 minutes until browned. Remove from heat and set aside.
3. **Cook the Vegetables:** Add mushrooms, onions, and garlic to the griddle. Cook for about 5 minutes until tender.
4. **Prepare the Sauce:** Add beef broth to the vegetables and let it simmer for 2 minutes. Stir in sour cream until well combined.
5. **Combine:** Return the beef to the griddle and mix with the sauce and vegetables. Cook for an additional 2-3 minutes.
6. Serve the beef stroganoff over cooked egg noodles if desired.

Serving Suggestions:
1. Serve with a side of steamed vegetables or a green salad.

Nutritional value (per serving)
Calories: 500 | Protein: 35g | Carbohydrates: 30g | Fats: 25g | Fiber: 4g

18. Tex-Mex Beef Nachos with Jalapeños

Difficulty Level: Easy | Prep Time: 10 minutes | Cooking Time: 10 minutes
Total Time: 20 minutes | Temperature: Medium-High Heat | Cooking Type: Griddling | Servings: 1 person

Ingredients:
- 4 oz ground beef
- 1/4 cup canned black beans, drained and rinsed
- 1/2 cup shredded cheddar cheese
- 1/4 cup sliced jalapeños
- 1/2 cup tortilla chips
- 1 tbsp olive oil
- Salt and pepper to taste

Instructions:
1. **Preheat the Griddle:** Set your gas griddle to medium-high heat.
2. **Cook the Beef:** Drizzle olive oil on the griddle. Add ground beef, salt, and pepper. Cook for about 5 minutes until browned. Add black beans and cook for an additional 2 minutes.
3. **Assemble the Nachos:** Arrange tortilla chips on a plate. Top with the beef and bean mixture, then sprinkle with cheddar cheese and sliced jalapeños.
4. **Melt the Cheese:** Place the plate on the griddle and cover with a lid to melt the cheese for about 2-3 minutes.
5. **Serve:** Remove from heat and serve immediately.

Serving Suggestions:
1. Serve with a side of salsa, guacamole, or sour cream.

Nutritional value (per serving)
Calories: 400 | Protein: 25g | Carbohydrates: 40g | Fats: 18g | Fiber: 6g

19. Southwestern Beef Enchiladas

- **Difficulty Level:** Medium
- **Prep Time:** 15 minutes
- **Cooking Time:** 20 minutes
- **Total Time:** 35 minutes
- **Temperature:** Medium-High Heat
- **Cooking Type:** Griddling, Sautéing
- **Servings:** 1 person

Ingredients:
- 4 oz ground beef
- 1/4 cup canned black beans, drained and rinsed
- 1/2 cup shredded cheddar cheese
- 1/4 cup diced onions
- 1 garlic clove, minced
- 1/2 cup enchilada sauce
- 2 small flour tortillas
- 1 tbsp olive oil
- Salt and pepper to taste

Nutritional value (per serving):
Calories: 500 | Protein: 35g
Carbohydrates: 30g | Fats: 25g | Fiber: 4g

Instructions:
1. **Preheat the Griddle:** Set your gas griddle to medium-high heat.
2. **Cook the Beef:** Drizzle olive oil on the griddle. Add ground beef, onions, garlic, salt, and pepper. Cook for about 5 minutes until browned. Add black beans and cook for an additional 2 minutes.
3. **Assemble the Enchiladas:** Place a small amount of beef mixture and cheese in each tortilla. Roll them up and place them seam-side down on the griddle.
4. **Cook the Enchiladas:** Drizzle enchilada sauce over the top and sprinkle with remaining cheese. Cover with a lid and cook for 5-7 minutes until the cheese is melted and bubbly.
5. **Serve:** Remove from heat and serve immediately.

Serving Suggestions:
1. Serve with a side of Mexican rice and a small green salad.

LAMB

20. Lamb Meatballs with Mint Yogurt Sauce

- **Difficulty Level:** Medium
- **Prep Time:** 20 minutes
- **Cooking Time:** 15 minutes
- **Total Time:** 35 minutes
- **Temperature:** Medium Heat
- **Cooking Type:** Griddling, Sautéing
- **Servings:** 1 person

Ingredients:
- 4 oz ground lamb
- 1/4 cup breadcrumbs
- 1 egg, beaten
- 1 garlic clove, minced
- 1 tbsp chopped fresh mint
- 1 tsp ground cumin
- Salt and pepper to taste
- For Mint Yogurt Sauce:
- 1/4 cup Greek yogurt
- 1 tbsp chopped fresh mint
- 1 tsp lemon juice
- Salt to taste

Instructions:
1. **Preheat the Griddle:** Set your gas griddle to medium heat.
2. **Prepare the Meatballs:** In a bowl, mix ground lamb, breadcrumbs, beaten egg, minced garlic, chopped mint, cumin, salt, and pepper. Form into small meatballs.
3. **Cook the Meatballs:** Place the meatballs on the griddle and cook for about 7-8 minutes, turning occasionally, until browned and cooked through.
4. **Prepare the Mint Yogurt Sauce:** In a small bowl, mix Greek yogurt, chopped mint, lemon juice, and salt.
5. Serve the meatballs with mint yogurt sauce on the side.

Serving Suggestions:
1. Serve with a side of couscous or a mixed greens salad.

Nutritional value (per serving):
Calories: 400 | Protein: 28g
Carbohydrates: 12g | Fats: 25g | Fiber: 2g

21. Greek Lamb Gyros with Tzatziki

Difficulty Level: Medium | **Prep Time:** 15 minutes | **Cooking Time:** 10 minutes
Total Time: 25 minutes | **Temperature:** Medium-High Heat | **Cooking Type:** Griddling, Sautéing | **Servings:** 1 person

Ingredients:
- 4 oz lamb, thinly sliced
- 1 tbsp olive oil
- 1 tsp dried oregano
- 1 tsp garlic powder
- Salt and pepper to taste
- 1 pita bread
- 1/2 cup shredded lettuce
- 1/4 cup diced tomatoes
- 1/4 cup sliced red onion
- For Tzatziki Sauce:
- 1/4 cup Greek yogurt
- 1/4 cucumber, grated
- 1 garlic clove, minced
- 1 tsp lemon juice
- Salt to taste

Instructions:
1. **Preheat the Griddle:** Set your gas griddle to medium-high heat.
2. **Marinate the Lamb:** In a bowl, combine lamb slices, olive oil, oregano, garlic powder, salt, and pepper. Let it marinate for at least 30 minutes.
3. **Cook the Lamb:** Place the lamb on the griddle and sear for about 3-4 minutes per side until browned and cooked through.
4. **Prepare the Tzatziki Sauce:** In a small bowl, mix Greek yogurt, grated cucumber, minced garlic, lemon juice, and salt.
5. **Assemble the Gyro:** Warm the pita bread on the griddle for about 1 minute per side. Place the cooked lamb on the pita, top with shredded lettuce, diced tomatoes, sliced red onion, and drizzle with tzatziki sauce.

Serving Suggestions:
1. Serve with a side of Greek salad or roasted vegetables.

Nutritional value (per serving):
Calories: 450 | Protein: 25g
Carbohydrates: 30g | Fats: 25g | Fiber: 3g

22. Lamb and Potato Skillet

Difficulty Level: Medium | **Prep Time:** 10 minutes | **Cooking Time:** 20 minutes
Total Time: 30 minutes | **Temperature:** Medium-High Heat | **Cooking Type:** Griddling, Sautéing | **Servings:** 1 person

Ingredients:
- 4 oz lamb, diced
- 1 medium potato, diced
- 1/4 cup diced onions
- 1/2 bell pepper, diced
- 1 garlic clove, minced
- 1 tbsp olive oil
- 1 tsp dried thyme
- Salt and pepper to taste

Instructions:
1. **Preheat the Griddle:** Set your gas griddle to medium-high heat.
2. **Cook the Potatoes:** Drizzle olive oil on the griddle. Add diced potatoes and cook for about 10 minutes, stirring occasionally, until golden brown and tender.
3. **Add Vegetables:** Add diced onions, bell pepper, and minced garlic. Cook for an additional 5 minutes.
4. **Cook the Lamb:** Add the diced lamb, dried thyme, salt, and pepper. Cook for 5-7 minutes until the lamb is browned and cooked.
5. **Serve:** Mix everything together and serve immediately.

Serving Suggestions:
1. Serve with a side of roasted vegetables or a small salad.

Nutritional value (per serving):
Calories: 450 | Protein: 30g
Carbohydrates: 35g | Fats: 20g | Fiber: 5g

23. Lamb Souvlaki with Lemon Rice

Difficulty Level: Medium | **Prep Time:** 15 minutes | **Cooking Time:** 15 minutes
Total Time: 30 minutes | **Temperature:** Medium-High Heat | **Cooking Type:** Griddling, Sautéing | **Servings:** 1 person

Ingredients:
- 4 oz lamb, diced
- 1 tbsp olive oil
- 1 tbsp lemon juice
- 1 tsp dried oregano
- 1 garlic clove, minced
- Salt and pepper to taste

For Lemon Rice:
- 1/2 cup cooked rice
- 1 tsp lemon zest
- 1 tbsp lemon juice
- Salt to taste

Nutritional value (per serving):
Calories: 450 | Protein: 30g
Carbohydrates: 40g | Fats: 20g | Fiber: 3g

Instructions:
1. Preheat the Griddle: Set your gas griddle to medium-high heat.
2. Marinate the Lamb: In a bowl, combine lamb, olive oil, lemon juice, dried oregano, minced garlic, salt, and pepper. Let it marinate for at least 30 minutes.
3. Cook the Lamb: Place the marinated lamb on the griddle and sear for 3-4 minutes per side until browned and cooked.
4. Prepare the Lemon Rice: In a small bowl, mix cooked rice, lemon zest, lemon juice, and salt.
5. Serve the lamb souvlaki with lemon rice.

Serving Suggestions:
1. Serve with a side of Greek salad or tzatziki sauce.

24. Curried Lamb Skewers with Coconut Rice

Difficulty Level: Medium | **Prep Time:** 20 minutes | **Cooking Time:** 15 minutes
Total Time: 35 minutes | **Temperature:** Medium-High Heat | **Cooking Type:** Griddling, Sautéing | **Servings:** 1 person

Ingredients:
- 4 oz lamb, diced
- 1 tbsp curry powder
- 1 garlic clove, minced
- 1 tbsp olive oil
- 1 tsp salt

For Coconut Rice:
- 1/2 cup cooked rice
- 1/4 cup coconut milk
- 1 tbsp shredded coconut
- Salt to taste

Nutritional value (per serving):
Calories: 500 | Protein: 30g
Carbohydrates: 50g | Fats: 20g | Fiber: 4g

Instructions:
1. Preheat the Griddle: Set your gas griddle to medium-high heat.
2. Marinate the Lamb: In a bowl, combine lamb, curry powder, minced garlic, olive oil, and salt. Let it marinate for at least 30 minutes.
3. Assemble the Skewers: Thread the marinated lamb onto skewers.
4. Cook the Skewers: Place the skewers on the griddle and cook for 3-4 minutes per side until browned and cooked.
5. Prepare the Coconut Rice: Combine cooked rice, coconut milk, shredded coconut, and salt in a small saucepan. Heat until warm.
6. Serve the curried lamb skewers with coconut rice.

Serving Suggestions:
1. Serve with a side of cucumber salad or mango chutney.

25. Lamb Pita Pockets with Hummus

Difficulty Level: Easy | Prep Time: 10 minutes | Cooking Time: 10 minutes
Total Time: 20 minutes | Temperature: Medium-High Heat | Cooking Type: Griddling, Sautéing | Servings: 1 person

Ingredients:
- 4 oz lamb, thinly sliced
- 1 tbsp olive oil
- 1 tsp ground cumin
- 1/2 tsp ground coriander
- Salt and pepper to taste
- 1 pita bread
- 2 tbsp hummus
- 1/4 cup shredded lettuce
- 1/4 cup diced tomatoes
- 1/4 cup sliced cucumber

Instructions:
1. Preheat the Griddle: Set your gas griddle to medium-high heat.
2. Cook the Lamb: Drizzle olive oil on the griddle. Add lamb slices, cumin, coriander, salt, and pepper. Cook for 3-4 minutes per side until browned and cooked through.
3. Warm the Pita: Place the pita bread on the griddle for about 1 minute per side to warm it.
4. Assemble the Pita Pocket: Spread hummus inside the pita bread. Add the cooked lamb, shredded lettuce, diced tomatoes, and sliced cucumber.
5. Serve immediately.

Serving Suggestions:
1. Serve with a side of tabbouleh or Greek salad.

Nutritional value (per serving):
Calories: 400 | Protein: 25g | Carbohydrates: 35g | Fats: 18g | Fiber: 5g

PORK

26. BBQ Pulled Pork Sandwiches

Difficulty Level: Medium | Prep Time: 15 minutes | Cooking Time: 6 hours (slow cooker) + 10 minutes (griddle)
Total Time: 6 hours 25 minutes | Temperature: Medium Heat | Cooking Type: Griddling, Searing | Servings: 1 person

Ingredients:
- 4 oz pulled pork (prepared in a slow cooker with BBQ sauce)
- 1 hamburger bun
- 1/4 cup coleslaw
- 2 tbsp extra BBQ sauce
- 1 tbsp olive oil

Instructions:
1. Preheat the Griddle: Set your gas griddle to medium heat.
2. Reheat the Pulled Pork: Place the pulled pork on the griddle and drizzle with olive oil. Cook for about 5 minutes until heated through.
3. Toast the Bun: Place the hamburger bun on the griddle and toast for about 1 minute per side.
4. Assemble the Sandwich: Place the heated pulled pork on the bottom half of the bun, top with extra BBQ sauce and coleslaw, and place the top bun on.
5. Serve immediately.

Serving Suggestions:
1. Serve with a side of potato chips or a pickle.

Nutritional value (per serving):
Calories: 450 | Protein: 28g | Carbohydrates: 40g | Fats: 18g | Fiber: 3g

27. Sweet and Sour Pork Skewers

Difficulty Level: Medium | Prep Time: 20 minutes | Cooking Time: 10 minutes
Total Time: 30 minutes | Temperature: Medium-High Heat | Cooking Type: Griddling, Searing | Servings: 1 person

Ingredients:
- 4 oz pork tenderloin, cubed
- 1/4 cup pineapple chunks
- 1/4 cup bell pepper, cubed
- 1/4 cup onion, cubed
- 2 tbsp sweet and sour sauce
- 1 tbsp olive oil
- Salt and pepper to taste

Instructions:
1. Preheat the Griddle: Set your gas griddle to medium-high heat.
2. Assemble the Skewers: Thread the pork, pineapple, bell pepper, and onion onto skewers.
3. Cook the Skewers: Drizzle olive oil on the griddle. Place the skewers on the griddle and cook for about 8-10 minutes, turning occasionally, until the pork is cooked through and vegetables are tender.
4. Glaze with Sauce: Brush the skewers with sweet and sour sauce during the last 2 minutes of cooking.
5. Serve: Remove from heat and serve immediately.

Serving Suggestions:
1. Serve with a side of steamed rice or a green salad.

Nutritional value (per serving)
Calories: 350 | Protein: 25g | Carbohydrates: 30g | Fats: 12g | Fiber: 3g

28. Pork and Pineapple Fried Rice

Difficulty Level: Easy | Prep Time: 10 minutes | Cooking Time: 10 minutes
Total Time: 20 minutes | Temperature: Medium-High Heat | Cooking Type: Griddling, Sautéing | Servings: 1 person

Ingredients:
- 4 oz pork tenderloin, diced
- 1/4 cup pineapple chunks
- 1/2 cup cooked rice
- 1/4 cup diced bell pepper
- 1/4 cup diced onion
- 1 garlic clove, minced
- 2 tbsp soy sauce
- 1 tbsp olive oil
- Salt and pepper to taste

Instructions:
1. Preheat the Griddle: Set your gas griddle to medium-high heat.
2. Cook the Pork: Drizzle olive oil on the griddle. Add diced pork, salt, and pepper. Cook for about 5 minutes until browned.
3. Add Vegetables: Add pineapple, bell pepper, onion, and minced garlic. Cook for an additional 3-4 minutes.
4. Add Rice: Add cooked rice and soy sauce. Stir continuously for 2-3 minutes until everything is heated through and well mixed.
5. Serve: Remove from heat and serve immediately.

Serving Suggestions:
1. Serve with a side of steamed broccoli or a small salad.

Nutritional value (per serving)
Calories: 400 | Protein: 25g | Carbohydrates: 50g | Fats: 12g | Fiber: 4g

29. Crispy Pork Carnitas Tacos

- Difficulty Level: Medium
- Prep Time: 10 minutes
- Cooking Time: 20 minutes
- Total Time: 30 minutes
- Temperature: Medium-High Heat
- Cooking Type: Griddling, Searing
- Servings: 1 person

Ingredients:
- 4 oz shredded pork
- 2 small corn tortillas
- 1/4 cup diced onions
- 1/4 cup chopped cilantro
- 1 lime, cut into wedges
- 1 tbsp olive oil
- Salt and pepper to taste

Instructions:
1. Preheat the Griddle: Set your gas griddle to medium-high heat.
2. Cook the Pork: Drizzle olive oil on the griddle. Add shredded pork, salt, and pepper. Cook for about 5-7 minutes until crispy.
3. Warm the Tortillas: Place the tortillas on the griddle for about 1 minute per side to warm them.
4. Assemble the Tacos: Place the crispy pork on the tortillas and top with diced onions and chopped cilantro. Squeeze lime juice over the top.
5. Serve immediately.

Nutritional value (per serving):
Calories: 400 | Protein: 28g
Carbohydrates: 40g | Fats: 16g | Fiber: 4g

Serving Suggestions:
1. Serve with a side of salsa and guacamole.

30. Honey Garlic Pork Loin Medallions

- Difficulty Level: Medium
- Prep Time: 10 minutes
- Cooking Time: 15 minutes
- Total Time: 25 minutes
- Temperature: Medium Heat
- Cooking Type: Griddling, Searing
- Servings: 1 person

Ingredients:
- 4 oz pork loin, cut into medallions
- 1 tbsp honey
- 1 garlic clove, minced
- 1 tbsp soy sauce
- 1 tbsp olive oil
- Salt and pepper to taste

Instructions:
1. Preheat the Griddle: Set your gas griddle to medium heat.
2. Cook the Pork Medallions: Drizzle olive oil on the griddle. Season the pork medallions with salt and pepper. Cook for 5-6 minutes per side until browned and cooked through.
3. Add the Sauce: In the last 2 minutes of cooking, add honey, minced garlic, and soy sauce to the griddle. Coat the pork medallions with the sauce.
4. Serve: Let the pork medallions rest for a few minutes before serving.

Nutritional value (per serving):
Calories: 350 | Protein: 28g
Carbohydrates: 20g | Fats: 16g | Fiber: 1g

Serving Suggestions:
1. Serve with a side of steamed vegetables or rice.

31. Pork Fajitas with Bell Peppers

- Difficulty Level: Medium
- Prep Time: 15 minutes
- Cooking Time: 10 minutes
- Total Time: 25 minutes
- Temperature: Medium-High Heat
- Cooking Type: Griddling, Sautéing
- Servings: 1 person

Ingredients:
- 4 oz pork tenderloin, thinly sliced
- 1/2 bell pepper, sliced
- 1/4 cup sliced onions
- 1 garlic clove, minced
- 1 tbsp olive oil
- 1 tsp cumin
- 1 tsp chili powder
- Salt and pepper to taste
- 2 small flour tortillas

Instructions:
1. Preheat the Griddle: Set your gas griddle to medium-high heat.
2. Cook the Pork: Drizzle olive oil on the griddle. Add the pork, cumin, chili powder, salt, and pepper. Cook for about 5-7 minutes until browned.
3. Add Vegetables: Add sliced bell pepper, onions, and minced garlic. Cook for an additional 3-4 minutes until vegetables are tender.
4. Warm the Tortillas: Place the tortillas on the griddle for about 1 minute per side to warm them.
5. Assemble the Fajitas: Place the pork and vegetable mixture on the tortillas.
6. Serve immediately.

Serving Suggestions:
1. Serve with a side of salsa, guacamole, or sour cream.
2. Top of Form
3. Bottom of Form

Nutritional value (per serving):
Calories: 400 | Protein: 28g
Carbohydrates: 35g | Fats: 18g | Fiber: 4g

SAUCE

32. Smoky Chipotle BBQ Sauce

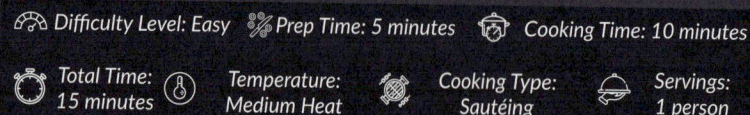

- Difficulty Level: Easy
- Prep Time: 5 minutes
- Cooking Time: 10 minutes
- Total Time: 15 minutes
- Temperature: Medium Heat
- Cooking Type: Sautéing
- Servings: 1 person

Ingredients:
- 1/2 cup ketchup
- 1 tbsp apple cider vinegar
- 1 tbsp brown sugar
- 1 tbsp molasses
- 1 chipotle pepper in adobo, minced
- 1 tsp smoked paprika
- 1 garlic clove, minced
- 1/2 tsp onion powder
- Salt and pepper to taste

Instructions:
1. Preheat the Griddle: Set your gas griddle to medium heat.
2. Mix Ingredients: In a small saucepan, combine ketchup, apple cider vinegar, brown sugar, molasses, minced chipotle pepper, smoked paprika, minced garlic, onion powder, salt, and pepper.
3. Cook the Sauce: Place the saucepan on the griddle and bring the mixture to a simmer. Cook for about 10 minutes, stirring frequently, until the sauce thickens.
4. Serve: Remove from heat and let cool slightly before serving.

Serving Suggestions:
1. Serve with grilled meats like chicken, pork, or beef.

Nutritional value (per serving):
Calories: 60 | Protein: 1g
Carbohydrates: 14g | Fats: 0g
Fiber: 1g

33. Creamy Garlic Herb Aioli

- Difficulty Level: Easy
- Prep Time: 5 minutes
- Cooking Time: 5 minutes
- Total Time: 10 minutes
- Temperature: Low Heat
- Cooking Type: Sautéing
- Servings: 1 person

Ingredients:
- 1/2 cup mayonnaise
- 1 garlic clove, minced
- 1 tbsp lemon juice
- 1 tsp Dijon mustard
- 1 tbsp chopped fresh parsley
- 1 tbsp chopped fresh chives
- Salt and pepper to taste

Instructions:
1. Preheat the Griddle: Set your gas griddle to low heat.
2. Prepare the Aioli: In a small bowl, mix mayonnaise, minced garlic, lemon juice, Dijon mustard, chopped parsley, chopped chives, salt, and pepper.
3. Mix Well: Stir until all ingredients are well combined.
4. Serve: Chill for at least 10 minutes before serving.

Serving Suggestions:
1. Serve with grilled vegetables, sandwiches, or as a dip for fries.

Nutritional value (per serving):
Calories: 100 | Protein: 1g
Carbohydrates: 1g | Fats: 10g
Fiber: 0g

34. Classic Marinara with Fresh Basil

- Difficulty Level: Medium
- Prep Time: 10 minutes
- Cooking Time: 20 minutes
- Total Time: 30 minutes
- Temperature: Medium Heat
- Cooking Type: Sautéing
- Servings: 1 person

Ingredients:
- 2 cups diced tomatoes
- 1/4 cup diced onions
- 2 garlic cloves, minced
- 1 tbsp olive oil
- 1 tsp dried oregano
- 1 tsp dried basil
- 1/4 cup fresh basil, chopped
- Salt and pepper to taste

Nutritional value (per serving):
Calories: 80 | Protein: 2g
Carbohydrates: 14g | Fats: 2g
Fiber: 3g

Instructions:
1. Preheat the Griddle: Set your gas griddle to medium heat.
2. Cook the Onions and Garlic: Drizzle olive oil on the griddle. Add diced onions and minced garlic. Sauté for about 5 minutes until softened.
3. Add Tomatoes and Herbs: Add diced tomatoes, dried oregano, dried basil, salt, and pepper. Cook for about 15 minutes, stirring occasionally.
4. Add Fresh Basil: Stir in chopped fresh basil and cook for 2 minutes.
5. Serve: Remove from heat and let cool slightly before serving.

Serving Suggestions:
1. Serve with pasta, meatballs, or as a pizza sauce.

35. Spicy Sriracha Mayo

Difficulty Level: Easy | Prep Time: 5 minutes | Cooking Time: 0 minutes
Total Time: 5 minutes | Temperature: None | Cooking Type: Mixing | Servings: 1 person

Ingredients:
- 1/4 cup mayonnaise
- 1 tbsp Sriracha sauce
- 1 tsp lemon juice
- Salt to taste

Instructions:
1. Mix Ingredients: In a small bowl, combine mayonnaise, Sriracha sauce, lemon juice, and salt.
2. Stir Well: Mix until all ingredients are well combined.
3. Serve immediately or chill for 10 minutes before serving.

Nutritional value (per serving):
Calories: 90 | Protein: 1g
Carbohydrates: 1g | Fats: 9g
Fiber: 0g

Serving Suggestions:
1. Serve with sandwiches, burgers, or as a dip for fries and vegetables.

36. Zesty Lemon Dill Sauce

Difficulty Level: Easy | Prep Time: 5 minutes | Cooking Time: 5 minutes
Total Time: 10 minutes | Temperature: Low Heat | Cooking Type: Sautéing | Servings: 1 person

Ingredients:
- 1/4 cup Greek yogurt
- 1 tbsp mayonnaise
- 1 tbsp lemon juice
- 1 tsp lemon zest
- 1 tbsp chopped fresh dill
- Salt and pepper to taste

Nutritional value (per serving):
Calories: 50 | Protein: 1g
Carbohydrates: 2g | Fats: 4g
Fiber: 0g

Instructions:
1. Preheat the Griddle: Set your gas griddle to low heat.
2. Mix Ingredients: In a small bowl, combine Greek yogurt, mayonnaise, lemon juice, lemon zest, chopped dill, salt, and pepper.
3. Warm the Sauce: Place the bowl on the griddle and warm the mixture, stirring constantly for about 5 minutes.
4. Serve: Remove from heat and let cool slightly before serving.

Serving Suggestions:
1. Serve with grilled fish or chicken or as a salad dressing.

37. Savory Mushroom Gravy

Difficulty Level: Medium | Prep Time: 10 minutes | Cooking Time: 15 minutes
Total Time: 25 minutes | Temperature: Medium Heat | Cooking Type: Sautéing | Servings: 1 person

Ingredients:
- 1/2 cup sliced mushrooms
- 1/4 cup diced onions
- 1 garlic clove, minced
- 1 tbsp butter
- 1 tbsp all-purpose flour
- 1/2 cup beef broth
- 1/4 cup heavy cream
- Salt and pepper to taste

Nutritional value (per serving):
Calories: 80 | Protein: 2g
Carbohydrates: 6g | Fats: 6g
Fiber: 1g

Instructions:
1. Preheat the Griddle: Set your gas griddle to medium heat.
2. Cook the Vegetables: Melt butter on the griddle. Add sliced mushrooms, diced onions, and minced garlic. Sauté for about 5 minutes until softened.
3. Make the Roux: Sprinkle flour over the vegetables and cook, stirring constantly, for about 2 minutes until the flour is golden brown.
4. Add Liquid: Gradually stir in beef broth and heavy cream. Cook, stirring constantly, for about 8 minutes until the gravy thickens.
5. Season: Add salt and pepper to taste.
6. Serve: Remove from heat and let cool slightly before serving.

Serving Suggestions:
1. Serve with mashed potatoes, meatloaf, or roasted meats.

VEGETABLES AND SIDE DISHES

38. Grilled Asparagus with Parmesan and Lemon

Difficulty Level: Easy | Prep Time: 5 minutes | Cooking Time: 10 minutes
Total Time: 15 minutes | Temperature: Medium-High Heat | Cooking Type: Griddling | Servings: 1 person

Ingredients:
- 1 cup asparagus spears, trimmed
- 1 tbsp olive oil
- 1 tbsp grated Parmesan cheese
- 1 tsp lemon zest
- Salt and pepper to taste

Nutritional value (per serving):
Calories: 90 | Protein: 4g
Carbohydrates: 6g | Fats: 6g
Fiber: 3g

Instructions:
1. Preheat the Griddle: Set your gas griddle to medium-high heat.
2. Prepare the Asparagus: Toss the asparagus in olive oil, salt, and pepper.
3. Grill the Asparagus: Place the asparagus on the griddle and cook for about 8-10 minutes, turning occasionally, until tender and slightly charred.
4. Finish with Parmesan and Lemon: Sprinkle the grated Parmesan and lemon zest over the asparagus.
5. Serve immediately.

Serving Suggestions:
1. Serve as a side dish with grilled chicken or fish.

39. Honey-Glazed Carrots with Thyme

Difficulty Level: Easy	Prep Time: 5 minutes	Cooking Time: 10 minutes
Total Time: 15 minutes	Temperature: Medium Heat	Cooking Type: Sautéing
Servings: 1 person		

Ingredients:
- ½ lb. young carrots
- 1 tbsp honey
- 1 tbsp butter
- 1 tsp fresh thyme leaves
- Salt and pepper to taste

Nutritional value (per serving):
Calories: 110 | Protein: 1g
Carbohydrates: 20g | Fats: 4g
Fiber: 3g

Instructions:
1. Preheat the Griddle: Set your gas griddle to medium heat.
2. Cook the Carrots: Melt butter on the griddle. Add baby carrots and sauté for about 8 minutes until tender.
3. Glaze the Carrots: Drizzle honey over the carrots and sprinkle with fresh thyme leaves. Cook for an additional 2 minutes, stirring frequently.
4. Serve: Season with salt and pepper, and serve immediately.

Serving Suggestions:
1. Serve as a side dish with roasted meats or fish.

40. Sautéed Brussels Sprouts with Bacon

Difficulty Level: Medium	Prep Time: 5 minutes	Cooking Time: 10 minutes
Total Time: 15 minutes	Temperature: Medium-High Heat	Cooking Type: Sautéing
Servings: 1 person		

Ingredients:
- 1 cup Brussels sprouts, halved
- 2 slices thick-cut bacon, diced
- 1 garlic clove, minced
- Salt and pepper to taste

Nutritional value (per serving):
Calories: 150 | Protein: 5g
Carbohydrates: 10g | Fats: 10g | Fiber: 4g

Instructions:
1. Preheat the Griddle: Set your gas griddle to medium-high heat.
2. Cook the Bacon: Add diced bacon to the griddle and cook until crispy. Remove and set aside.
3. Sauté the Brussels Sprouts: Add halved Brussels sprouts to the bacon fat and cook for about 8 minutes until tender and browned. Add minced garlic in the last 2 minutes.
4. Combine and Serve: Toss the Brussels sprouts with the cooked bacon. Season with salt and pepper, and serve immediately.

Serving Suggestions:
1. Serve as a side dish with grilled steak or chicken.

41. Charred Corn and Black Bean Salad

- Difficulty Level: Easy
- Prep Time: 10 minutes
- Cooking Time: 10 minutes
- Total Time: 20 minutes
- Temperature: Medium-High Heat
- Cooking Type: Griddling, Sautéing
- Servings: 1 person

Ingredients:
- 1 ear of corn, kernels removed
- 1/2 cup canned black beans, drained and rinsed
- 1/4 cup diced red bell pepper
- 1/4 cup diced red onion
- 1 tbsp olive oil
- 1 tbsp lime juice
- 1 tbsp chopped cilantro
- Salt and pepper to taste

Nutritional value (per serving):
Calories: 180 | Protein: 6g
Carbohydrates: 30g | Fats: 6g
Fiber: 7g

Instructions:
1. Preheat the Griddle: Set your gas griddle to medium-high heat.
2. Cook the Corn: Drizzle olive oil on the griddle. Add corn kernels and cook for about 5 minutes until slightly charred.
3. Add Vegetables: Add black beans, red bell pepper, and red onion. Cook for an additional 3 minutes.
4. Combine and Serve: Remove from heat and toss with lime juice and chopped cilantro. Season with salt and pepper, and serve immediately.

Serving Suggestions:
1. Serve as a side dish with grilled fish or chicken.

42. Garlic Butter Green Beans

- Difficulty Level: Easy
- Prep Time: 5 minutes
- Cooking Time: 10 minutes
- Total Time: 15 minutes
- Temperature: Medium Heat
- Cooking Type: Sautéing
- Servings: 1 person

Ingredients:
- 1 cup green beans, trimmed
- 1 tbsp butter
- 1 garlic clove, minced
- Salt and pepper to taste

Nutritional value (per serving):
Calories: 90 | Protein: 2g
Carbohydrates: 10g | Fats: 5g
Fiber: 4g

Instructions:
1. Preheat the Griddle: Set your gas griddle to medium heat.
2. Cook the Green Beans: Melt butter on the griddle. Add green beans and sauté for about 8 minutes until tender.
3. Add Garlic: Add minced garlic and cook for an additional 2 minutes.
4. Serve: Season with salt and pepper, and serve immediately.

Serving Suggestions:
1. Serve as a side dish with grilled chicken or pork.

43. Spicy Roasted Cauliflower

- Difficulty Level: Easy
- Prep Time: 5 minutes
- Cooking Time: 15 minutes
- Total Time: 20 minutes
- Temperature: Medium-High Heat
- Cooking Type: Griddling, Searing
- Servings: 1 person

Ingredients:
- 1 cup cauliflower florets
- 1 tbsp olive oil
- 1/2 tsp smoked paprika
- 1/2 tsp chili powder
- Salt and pepper to taste

Nutritional value (per serving):
Calories: 80 | Protein: 3g
Carbohydrates: 10g | Fats: 4g
Fiber: 3g

Instructions:
1. Preheat the Griddle: Set your gas griddle to medium-high heat.
2. Prepare the Cauliflower: Toss cauliflower florets in olive oil, smoked paprika, chili powder, salt, and pepper.
3. Roast the Cauliflower: Place the cauliflower on the griddle and cook for about 15 minutes, stirring occasionally, until tender and slightly charred.
4. Serve immediately.

Serving Suggestions:
1. Serve as a side dish with grilled steak or chicken.

44. Stuffed Portobello Mushrooms with Spinach and Feta

- Difficulty Level: Medium
- Prep Time: 10 minutes
- Cooking Time: 15 minutes
- Total Time: 25 minutes
- Temperature: Medium Heat
- Cooking Type: Griddling, Sautéing
- Servings: 1 person

Ingredients:
- 1 large portobello mushroom
- 1 cup fresh spinach, chopped
- 1/4 cup crumbled feta cheese
- 1 garlic clove, minced
- 1 tbsp olive oil
- Salt and pepper to taste

Nutritional value (per serving):
Calories: 150 | Protein: 8g
Carbohydrates: 10g | Fats: 9g
Fiber: 3g

Instructions:
1. Preheat the Griddle: Set your gas griddle to medium heat.
2. Cook the Spinach: Drizzle olive oil on the griddle. Add chopped spinach and minced garlic. Sauté for about 5 minutes until the spinach is wilted.
3. Stuff the Mushroom: Remove the gills from the portobello mushroom. Stuff with the cooked spinach and top with crumbled feta cheese.
4. Grill the Mushroom: Place the stuffed mushroom on the griddle and cook for 10 minutes until tender and the cheese is melted.
5. Serve: Season with salt and pepper, and serve immediately.

Serving Suggestions:
1. Serve as a side dish with grilled chicken or fish.

45. Crispy Herb-Roasted Potatoes

Difficulty Level: Easy | **Prep Time:** 5 minutes | **Cooking Time:** 20 minutes
Total Time: 25 minutes | **Temperature:** Medium-High Heat | **Cooking Type:** Griddling, Searing | **Servings:** 1 person

Ingredients:
- 1 cup diced potatoes
- 1 tbsp olive oil
- 1 tsp dried rosemary
- 1 tsp dried thyme
- Salt and pepper to taste

Nutritional value (per serving):
Calories: 200 | Protein: 3g
Carbohydrates: 36g | Fats: 6g
Fiber: 4g

Instructions:
1. Preheat the Griddle: Set your gas griddle to medium-high heat.
2. Prepare the Potatoes: Toss diced potatoes in olive oil, dried rosemary, dried thyme, salt, and pepper.
3. Roast the Potatoes: Place the potatoes on the griddle and cook for about 20 minutes, stirring occasionally, until crispy and golden brown.
4. Serve immediately.

Serving Suggestions:
1. Serve as a side dish with grilled steak or chicken.

46. Loaded Baked Potato Skins

Difficulty Level: Medium | **Prep Time:** 10 minutes | **Cooking Time:** 15 minutes
Total Time: 25 minutes | **Temperature:** Medium-High Heat | **Cooking Type:** Griddling, Searing | **Servings:** 1 person

Ingredients:
- 1 baked potato, halved
- 1/4 cup shredded cheddar cheese
- 2 slices cooked bacon, crumbled
- 1 tbsp sour cream
- 1 tbsp chopped green onions
- Salt and pepper to taste

Nutritional value (per serving):
Calories: 250 | Protein: 8g
Carbohydrates: 30g | Fats: 12g | Fiber: 4g

Instructions:
1. Preheat the Griddle: Set your gas griddle to medium-high heat.
2. Prepare the Potato Skins: Scoop out the center of the baked potato halves, leaving a small potato border. Brush with olive oil and season with salt and pepper.
3. Crisp the Skins: Place the potato skins on the griddle, cut side down, and cook for about 5 minutes until crispy.
4. Add Toppings: Turn the skins over and sprinkle with shredded cheddar cheese and crumbled bacon. Cook for an additional 5 minutes until the cheese is melted.
5. Serve: Top with sour cream and chopped green onions.

Serving Suggestions:
1. Serve as an appetizer or side dish with a salad.

47. Southwest Quinoa Salad

Difficulty Level: Easy	Prep Time: 10 minutes	Cooking Time: 10 minutes
Total Time: 20 minutes	Temperature: Medium Heat	Cooking Type: Sautéing	Servings: 1 person

Ingredients:
- 1/2 cup cooked quinoa
- 1/4 cup canned black beans, drained and rinsed
- 1/4 cup corn kernels
- 1/4 cup diced red bell pepper
- 1/4 cup diced red onion
- 1 tbsp olive oil
- 1 tbsp lime juice
- 1 tbsp chopped cilantro
- 1 tsp cumin
- Salt and pepper to taste

Instructions:
1. Preheat the Griddle: Set your gas griddle to medium heat.
2. Cook the Vegetables: Drizzle olive oil on the griddle. Add corn, red bell pepper, and red onion. Sauté for about 5 minutes until tender.
3. Add Quinoa and Beans: Add cooked quinoa, black beans, lime juice, chopped cilantro, cumin, salt, and pepper. Cook for an additional 3-5 minutes, stirring frequently.
4. Serve immediately.

Serving Suggestions:
1. Serve as a primary or side dish with grilled chicken or fish.

Nutritional value (per serving):
Calories: 220 | Protein: 8g
Carbohydrates: 30g | Fats: 8g
Fiber: 6g

BURGER RECIPES

48. Classic All-American Cheeseburger

Difficulty Level: Easy	Prep Time: 5 minutes	Cooking Time: 10 minutes
Total Time: 15 minutes	Temperature: Medium-High Heat	Cooking Type: Griddling, Searing	Servings: 1 person

Ingredients:
- 4 oz ground beef patty
- 1 slice of American cheese
- 1 hamburger bun
- 1 tbsp olive oil
- Salt and pepper to taste
- 1 leaf lettuce
- 1 slice tomato
- 1 slice red onion
- 1 tbsp ketchup
- 1 tbsp mustard

Instructions:
1. Preheat the Griddle: Set your gas griddle to medium-high heat.
2. Season the Patty: Season the ground beef patty with salt and pepper.
3. Cook the Patty: Drizzle olive oil on the griddle. Place the patty on the griddle and cook for about 4-5 minutes per side until browned and cooked through.
4. Add Cheese: Place a slice of American cheese on the patty in the last minute of cooking to melt.
5. Toast the Bun: Place the hamburger bun on the griddle, cut side down, and toast for about 1 minute.
6. Assemble the Burger: Place the lettuce, tomato, and red onion on the bottom bun. Add the patty with melted cheese. Spread ketchup and mustard on the top bun and place it on top.
7. Serve immediately.

Serving Suggestions:
1. Serve with a side of French fries or a small salad.

Nutritional value (per serving):
Calories: 500 | Protein: 30g
Carbohydrates: 35g | Fats: 25g | Fiber: 2g

49. Smoky BBQ Bacon Burger

Difficulty Level: Medium | Prep Time: 5 minutes | Cooking Time: 15 minutes
Total Time: 20 minutes | Temperature: Medium-High Heat | Cooking Type: Griddling, Searing | Servings: 1 person

Ingredients:
- 4 oz ground beef patty
- 2 slices thick-cut bacon
- 1 slice of cheddar cheese
- 1 hamburger bun
- 1 tbsp olive oil
- 2 tbsp BBQ sauce
- Salt and pepper to taste
- 1 leaf lettuce
- 1 slice tomato

Nutritional value (per serving):
Calories: 600 | Protein: 35g | Carbohydrates: 35g | Fats: 35g | Fiber: 2g

Instructions:
1. **Preheat the Griddle:** Set your gas griddle to medium-high heat.
2. **Cook the Bacon:** Place the bacon slices on the griddle and cook until crispy. Remove and set aside.
3. **Season the Patty:** Season the ground beef patty with salt and pepper.
4. **Cook the Patty:** Drizzle olive oil on the griddle. Place the patty on the griddle and cook for about 4-5 minutes per side until browned and cooked through.
5. **Add Cheese and Sauce:** In the last minute of cooking, place a slice of cheddar cheese on the patty to melt. Brush the patty with BBQ sauce.
6. **Toast the Bun:** Place the hamburger bun on the griddle, cut side down, and toast for about 1 minute.
7. **Assemble the Burger:** Place the lettuce and tomato on the bottom bun. Add the patty with melted cheese and BBQ sauce. Top with crispy bacon and the top bun.
8. Serve immediately.

Serving Suggestions:
1. Serve with a side of coleslaw or sweet potato fries.

50. Spicy Jalapeño Pepper Jack Burger

Difficulty Level: Medium | Prep Time: 5 minutes | Cooking Time: 10 minutes
Total Time: 15 minutes | Temperature: Medium-High Heat | Cooking Type: Griddling, Searing | Servings: 1 person

Ingredients:
- 4 oz ground beef patty
- 1 slice pepper jack cheese
- 1 hamburger bun
- 1 tbsp olive oil
- 1 jalapeño, sliced
- Salt and pepper to taste
- 1 leaf lettuce
- 1 slice tomato
- 1 tbsp spicy mayo (mayonnaise mixed with Sriracha sauce)

Nutritional value (per serving):
Calories: 550 | Protein: 32g | Carbohydrates: 35g | Fats: 30g | Fiber: 3g

Instructions:
1. **Preheat the Griddle:** Set your gas griddle to medium-high heat.
2. **Season the Patty:** Season the ground beef patty with salt and pepper.
3. **Cook the Patty:** Drizzle olive oil on the griddle. Place the patty on the griddle and cook for about 4-5 minutes per side until browned and cooked through.
4. **Add Cheese and Jalapeños:** In the last minute of cooking, place a slice of pepper jack cheese on the patty to melt. Slice jalapeños on top.
5. **Toast the Bun:** Place the hamburger bun on the griddle, cut side down, and toast for about 1 minute.
6. **Assemble the Burger:** Spread spicy mayo on the bottom bun. Place the lettuce and tomato on the bottom bun. Add the patty with melted cheese and jalapeños. Top with the top bun.
7. Serve immediately.

Serving Suggestions:
1. Serve with a side of onion rings or a small green salad.

51. Mushroom Swiss Burger with Caramelized Onions

Difficulty Level: Medium | **Prep Time:** 10 minutes | **Cooking Time:** 15 minutes
Total Time: 25 minutes | **Temperature:** Medium Heat | **Cooking Type:** Griddling, Searing, Sautéing | **Servings:** 1 person

Ingredients:
- 4 oz ground beef patty
- 1 slice Swiss cheese
- 1 hamburger bun
- 1 tbsp olive oil
- 1/2 cup sliced mushrooms
- 1/2 cup sliced onions
- 1 tbsp butter
- Salt and pepper to taste
- 1 tbsp mayonnaise

Nutritional value (per serving):
Calories: 600 | Protein: 30g | Carbohydrates: 40g | Fats: 35g | Fiber: 3g

Instructions:
1. **Preheat the Griddle:** Set your gas griddle to medium heat.
2. **Cook the Onions and Mushrooms:** Melt butter on the griddle. Add sliced onions and mushrooms. Sauté for about 10-12 minutes until caramelized and tender. Remove and set aside.
3. **Season the Patty:** Season the ground beef patty with salt and pepper.
4. **Cook the Patty:** Drizzle olive oil on the griddle. Place the patty on the griddle and cook for about 4-5 minutes per side until browned and cooked through.
5. **Add Cheese:** Place a slice of Swiss cheese on the patty in the last minute of cooking to melt.
6. **Toast the Bun:** Place the hamburger bun on the griddle, cut side down, and toast for about 1 minute.
7. **Assemble the Burger:** Spread mayonnaise on the bottom bun. Add the patty with melted cheese. Top with caramelized onions and mushrooms. Place the top bun on.
8. **Serve immediately.**

Serving Suggestions:
1. Serve with a side of garlic fries or a small green salad.

52. Avocado Bacon Ranch Burger

Difficulty Level: Medium | **Prep Time:** 5 minutes | **Cooking Time:** 15 minutes
Total Time: 20 minutes | **Temperature:** Medium-High Heat | **Cooking Type:** Griddling, Searing | **Servings:** 1 person

Ingredients:
- 4 oz ground beef patty
- 2 slices thick-cut bacon
- 1/2 avocado, sliced
- 1 slice of cheddar cheese
- 1 hamburger bun
- 1 tbsp olive oil
- 1 tbsp ranch dressing
- Salt and pepper to taste
- 1 leaf lettuce
- 1 slice tomato

Nutritional value (per serving):
Calories: 650 | Protein: 35g | Carbohydrates: 35g | Fats: 40g | Fiber: 6g

Instructions:
1. **Preheat the Griddle:** Set your gas griddle to medium-high heat.
2. **Cook the Bacon:** Place the bacon slices on the griddle and cook until crispy. Remove and set aside.
3. **Season the Patty:** Season the ground beef patty with salt and pepper.
4. **Cook the Patty:** Drizzle olive oil on the griddle. Place the patty on the griddle and cook for about 4-5 minutes per side until browned and cooked through.
5. **Add Cheese:** Place a slice of cheddar cheese on the patty in the last minute of cooking to melt.
6. **Toast the Bun:** Place the hamburger bun on the griddle, cut side down, and toast for about 1 minute.
7. **Assemble the Burger:** Spread ranch dressing on the bottom bun. Place the lettuce and tomato on the bottom bun. Add the patty with melted cheese. Top with crispy bacon and avocado slices. Place the top bun on.
8. **Serve immediately.**

Serving Suggestions:
1. Serve with a side of sweet potato fries or a small salad.

53. Blue Cheese and Caramelized Onion Burger

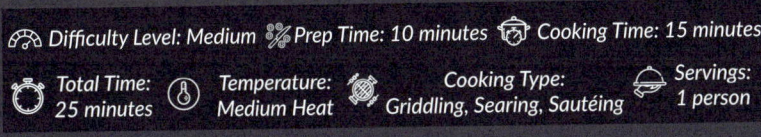

- Difficulty Level: Medium
- Prep Time: 10 minutes
- Cooking Time: 15 minutes
- Total Time: 25 minutes
- Temperature: Medium Heat
- Cooking Type: Griddling, Searing, Sautéing
- Servings: 1 person

Ingredients:
- 4 oz ground beef patty
- 1/4 cup crumbled blue cheese
- 1 hamburger bun
- 1 tbsp olive oil
- 1/2 cup sliced onions
- 1 tbsp butter
- Salt and pepper to taste
- 1 tbsp mayonnaise

Nutritional value (per serving):
Calories: 600 | Protein: 30g | Carbohydrates: 35g | Fats: 35g | Fiber: 3g

Instructions:
1. Preheat the Griddle: Set your gas griddle to medium heat.
2. Cook the Onions: Melt butter on the griddle. Add sliced onions and cook for 10-12 minutes until caramelized and tender. Remove and set aside.
3. Season the Patty: Season the ground beef patty with salt and pepper.
4. Cook the Patty: Drizzle olive oil on the griddle. Place the patty on the griddle and cook for about 4-5 minutes per side until browned and cooked through.
5. Add Blue Cheese: Sprinkle crumbled blue cheese on the patty in the last minute of cooking to melt.
6. Toast the Bun: Place the hamburger bun on the griddle, cut side down, and toast for about 1 minute.
7. Assemble the Burger: Spread mayonnaise on the bottom bun. Add the patty with melted blue cheese. Top with caramelized onions. Place the top bun on.
8. Serve immediately.

Serving Suggestions:
1. Serve with a side of garlic fries or a small green salad.

54. Hawaiian Teriyaki Pineapple Burger

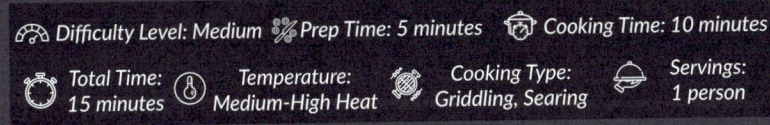

- Difficulty Level: Medium
- Prep Time: 5 minutes
- Cooking Time: 10 minutes
- Total Time: 15 minutes
- Temperature: Medium-High Heat
- Cooking Type: Griddling, Searing
- Servings: 1 person

Ingredients:
- 4 oz ground beef patty
- 1 slice Swiss cheese
- 1 hamburger bun
- 1 tbsp olive oil
- 1 pineapple ring
- 2 tbsp teriyaki sauce
- Salt and pepper to taste
- 1 leaf lettuce
- 1 slice tomato

Nutritional value (per serving):
Calories: 550 | Protein: 30g | Carbohydrates: 40g | Fats: 25g | Fiber: 3g

Instructions:
1. Preheat the Griddle: Set your gas griddle to medium-high heat.
2. Season the Patty: Season the ground beef patty with salt and pepper.
3. Cook the Patty: Drizzle olive oil on the griddle. Place the patty on the griddle and cook for about 4-5 minutes per side until browned and cooked through.
4. Add Cheese and Teriyaki Sauce: In the last minute of cooking, place a slice of Swiss cheese on the patty to melt. Brush the patty with teriyaki sauce.
5. Grill the Pineapple: Place the pineapple ring on the griddle and cook for 2 minutes per side until caramelized.
6. Toast the Bun: Place the hamburger bun on the griddle, cut side down, and toast for about 1 minute.
7. Assemble the Burger: Place the lettuce and tomato on the bottom bun. Add the patty with melted cheese and teriyaki sauce. Top with grilled pineapple. Place the top bun on.
8. Serve immediately.

Serving Suggestions:
1. Serve with a side of sweet potato fries or a small salad.

55. Tex-Mex Guacamole Burger

- Difficulty Level: Medium
- Prep Time: 10 minutes
- Cooking Time: 10 minutes
- Total Time: 20 minutes
- Temperature: Medium-High Heat
- Cooking Type: Griddling, Searing
- Servings: 1 person

Ingredients:

For the Burger:
- 4 oz ground beef patty
- 1 slice pepper jack cheese
- 1 hamburger bun
- 1 tbsp olive oil
- Salt and pepper to taste
- 1 leaf lettuce
- 1 slice tomato

For the Guacamole:
- 1/2 avocado, mashed
- 1 tbsp diced red onion
- 1 tbsp chopped cilantro
- 1/2 lime, juiced
- 1 small jalapeño, finely chopped (optional)
- Salt and pepper to taste

Nutritional value (per serving):
Calories: 600 | Protein: 32g
Carbohydrates: 40g | Fats: 35g | Fiber: 7g

Instructions:
1. Preheat the Griddle: Set your gas griddle to medium-high heat.
2. Prepare the Guacamole: In a small bowl, combine mashed avocado, diced red onion, chopped cilantro, lime juice, jalapeño (if using), salt, and pepper. Mix well and set aside.
3. Season the Patty: Season the ground beef patty with salt and pepper.
4. Cook the Patty: Drizzle olive oil on the griddle. Place the patty on the griddle and cook for about 4-5 minutes per side until browned and cooked through.
5. Add Cheese: In the last minute of cooking, place a slice of pepper jack cheese on the patty to melt.
6. Toast the Bun: Place the hamburger bun on the griddle, cut side down, and toast for about 1 minute.
7. Assemble the Burger: Place the lettuce and tomato on the bottom bun. Add the patty with melted cheese. Top with a generous spoonful of guacamole. Place the top bun on.
8. Serve immediately.

Serving Suggestions:
1. Serve with a side of tortilla chips and salsa.

56. Garlic Parmesan Turkey Burger

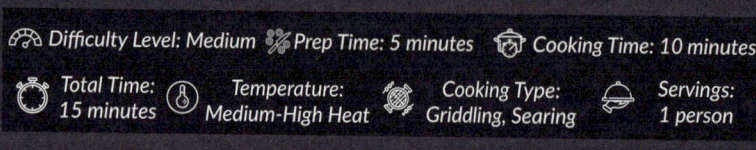

- Difficulty Level: Medium
- Prep Time: 5 minutes
- Cooking Time: 10 minutes
- Total Time: 15 minutes
- Temperature: Medium-High Heat
- Cooking Type: Griddling, Searing
- Servings: 1 person

Ingredients:
- 4 oz ground turkey patty
- 1 tbsp grated Parmesan cheese
- 1 garlic clove, minced
- 1 slice provolone cheese
- 1 hamburger bun
- 1 tbsp olive oil
- Salt and pepper to taste
- 1 leaf lettuce
- 1 slice tomato

Nutritional value (per serving):
Calories: 450 | Protein: 35g
Carbohydrates: 30g | Fats: 18g | Fiber: 2g

Instructions:
1. Preheat the Griddle: Set your gas griddle to medium-high heat.
2. Prepare the Patty: Mix ground turkey with grated Parmesan cheese, minced garlic, salt, and pepper. Form into a patty.
3. Cook the Patty: Drizzle olive oil on the griddle. Place the turkey patty on the griddle and cook for about 4-5 minutes per side until browned and cooked through.
4. Add Cheese: Place a slice of provolone cheese on the patty in the last minute of cooking to melt.
5. Toast the Bun: Place the hamburger bun on the griddle, cut side down, and toast for about 1 minute.
6. Assemble the Burger: Place the lettuce and tomato on the bottom bun. Add the patty with melted cheese. Place the top bun on.
7. Serve immediately.

Serving Suggestions:
1. Serve with a side of roasted vegetables or a small green salad.

57. Mediterranean Lamb Burger with Tzatziki

Difficulty Level: Medium   **Prep Time:** 10 minutes   **Cooking Time:** 10 minutes
Total Time: 20 minutes   **Temperature:** Medium-High Heat   **Cooking Type:** Griddling, Searing   **Servings:** 1 person

Ingredients:

For the Burger:
- 4 oz ground lamb patty
- 1 slice of feta cheese
- 1 hamburger bun
- 1 tbsp olive oil
- Salt and pepper to taste
- 1 leaf lettuce
- 1 slice tomato

For the Tzatziki Sauce:
- 1/4 cup Greek yogurt
- 1/4 cucumber, grated and drained
- 1 garlic clove, minced
- 1 tbsp chopped fresh dill
- 1/2 lemon, juiced
- Salt and pepper to taste

Nutritional value (per serving):
Calories: 600 | Protein: 30g
Carbohydrates: 35g | Fats: 35g | Fiber: 3g

Instructions:
1. Preheat the Griddle: Set your gas griddle to medium-high heat.
2. Prepare the Tzatziki Sauce: In a small bowl, combine Greek yogurt, grated cucumber, minced garlic, chopped dill, lemon juice, salt, and pepper. Mix well and set aside.
3. Season the Patty: Season the ground lamb patty with salt and pepper.
4. Cook the Patty: Drizzle olive oil on the griddle. Place the lamb patty on the griddle and cook for about 4-5 minutes per side until browned and cooked through.
5. Add Cheese: In the last minute of cooking, place a slice of feta cheese on the patty to melt slightly.
6. Toast the Bun: Place the hamburger bun on the griddle, cut side down, and toast for about 1 minute.
7. Assemble the Burger: Place the lettuce and tomato on the bottom bun. Add the patty with melted feta cheese. Top with a generous spoonful of tzatziki sauce. Place the top bun on.
8. Serve immediately.

Serving Suggestions:
1. Serve with a side of Greek salad or roasted vegetables.

58. Pesto Chicken Caprese Burger

Difficulty Level: Medium   **Prep Time:** 10 minutes   **Cooking Time:** 10 minutes
Total Time: 20 minutes   **Temperature:** Medium-High Heat   **Cooking Type:** Griddling, Searing   **Servings:** 1 person

Ingredients:
- 4 oz ground chicken patty
- 1 slice of fresh mozzarella cheese
- 1 hamburger bun
- 1 tbsp olive oil
- 1 tbsp basil pesto
- 1 slice tomato
- Salt and pepper to taste
- Fresh basil leaves

Nutritional value (per serving):
Calories: 500 | Protein: 35g
Carbohydrates: 30g | Fats: 22g | Fiber: 2g

Instructions:
1. Preheat the Griddle: Set your gas griddle to medium-high heat.
2. Season the Patty: Season the ground chicken patty with salt and pepper.
3. Cook the Patty: Drizzle olive oil on the griddle. Place the chicken patty on the griddle and cook for about 4-5 minutes per side until browned and cooked through.
4. Add Cheese: In the last minute of cooking, place a slice of fresh mozzarella cheese on the patty to melt slightly.
5. Toast the Bun: Place the hamburger bun on the griddle, cut side down, and toast for about 1 minute.
6. Assemble the Burger: Spread basil pesto on the bottom bun. Add the patty with melted mozzarella cheese. Top with a slice of tomato and fresh basil leaves. Place the top bun on.
7. Serve immediately.

Serving Suggestions:
1. Serve with a side of Caprese salad or roasted vegetables.

59. Chipotle Black Bean Veggie Burger

- Difficulty Level: Medium
- Prep Time: 15 minutes
- Cooking Time: 10 minutes
- Total Time: 25 minutes
- Temperature: Medium-High Heat
- Cooking Type: Griddling, Searing
- Servings: 1 person

Ingredients:

For the Patty:
- 1/2 cup canned black beans, drained and rinsed
- 1/4 cup breadcrumbs
- 1/4 cup finely chopped red bell pepper
- 1/4 cup finely chopped red onion
- 1 garlic clove, minced
- 1 chipotle pepper in adobo sauce, minced
- 1 tbsp adobo sauce
- 1 tsp cumin
- 1/2 tsp smoked paprika
- Salt and pepper to taste

For the Burger:
- 1 slice pepper jack cheese
- 1 hamburger bun
- 1 tbsp olive oil
- 1/4 cup guacamole
- 1 leaf lettuce
- 1 slice tomato

Instructions:

1. Prepare the Patty Mixture: In a bowl, mash the black beans with a fork until mostly smooth. Add breadcrumbs, chopped red bell pepper, chopped red onion, minced garlic, minced chipotle pepper, adobo sauce, cumin, smoked paprika, salt, and pepper. Mix until well combined.
2. Form the Patty: Shape the mixture into a patty, ensuring it is compact and holds together well.
3. Preheat the Griddle: Set your gas griddle to medium-high heat.
4. Cook the Patty: Drizzle olive oil on the griddle. Place the black bean patty on the griddle and cook for about 4-5 minutes per side until browned and heated through.
5. Add Cheese: In the last minute of cooking, place a slice of pepper jack cheese on the patty to melt.
6. Toast the Bun: Place the hamburger bun on the griddle, cut side down, and toast for about 1 minute.
7. Assemble the Burger: Place the lettuce and tomato on the bottom bun. Add the patty with melted cheese. Top with a generous spoonful of guacamole. Place the top bun on.
8. Serve immediately.

Serving Suggestions:
1. Serve with a side of sweet potato fries or a small salad.

Nutritional value (per serving):

Calories: 400 | Protein: 20g
Carbohydrates: 50g | Fats: 15g
Fiber: 15g

60. Spicy Sriracha Salmon Burger

- Difficulty Level: Medium
- Prep Time: 10 minutes
- Cooking Time: 10 minutes
- Total Time: 20 minutes
- Temperature: Medium-High Heat
- Cooking Type: Griddling, Searing
- Servings: 1 person

Ingredients:

- 4 oz salmon fillet, skin removed
- 1 tbsp Sriracha sauce
- 1 hamburger bun
- 1 tbsp olive oil
- Salt and pepper to taste
- 1 tbsp spicy mayo (mayonnaise mixed with Sriracha sauce)
- 1 slice tomato
- Fresh arugula

Nutritional value (per serving):

Calories: 400 | Protein: 30g
Carbohydrates: 25g | Fats: 20g | Fiber: 2g

Instructions:

1. Preheat the Griddle: Set your gas griddle to medium-high heat.
2. Prepare the Patty: Finely chop the salmon fillet and mix it with Sriracha sauce, salt, and pepper. Form into a patty.
3. Cook the Patty: Drizzle olive oil on the griddle. Place the salmon patty on the griddle and cook for about 4-5 minutes per side until browned and cooked through.
4. Toast the Bun: Place the hamburger bun on the griddle, cut side down, and toast for about 1 minute.
5. Assemble the Burger: Spread spicy mayo on the bottom bun. Add the patty. Top with a slice of tomato and fresh arugula. Place the top bun on.
6. Serve immediately.

Serving Suggestions:
1. Serve with a side of roasted sweet potatoes or a small salad.

61. Greek Feta and Spinach Burger

- Difficulty Level: Medium
- Prep Time: 10 minutes
- Cooking Time: 10 minutes
- Total Time: 20 minutes
- Temperature: Medium-High Heat
- Cooking Type: Griddling, Searing
- Servings: 1 person

Ingredients:
- 4 oz ground turkey patty
- 1/4 cup chopped fresh spinach
- 1/4 cup crumbled feta cheese
- 1 hamburger bun
- 1 tbsp olive oil
- Salt and pepper to taste
- 1 tbsp tzatziki sauce
- 1 slice tomato

Nutritional value (per serving):
Calories: 450 | Protein: 30g | Carbohydrates: 30g | Fats: 20g | Fiber: 3g

Instructions:
1. Preheat the Griddle: Set your gas griddle to medium-high heat.
2. Prepare the Patty: Mix ground turkey with chopped spinach, crumbled feta cheese, salt, and pepper. Form into a patty.
3. Cook the Patty: Drizzle olive oil on the griddle. Place the turkey patty on the griddle and cook for about 4-5 minutes per side until browned and cooked through.
4. Toast the Bun: Place the hamburger bun on the griddle, cut side down, and toast for about 1 minute.
5. Assemble the Burger: Spread tzatziki sauce on the bottom bun. Add the patty. Top with a slice of tomato. Place the top bun on.
6. Serve immediately.

Serving Suggestions:
1. Serve with a side of Greek salad or roasted vegetables.

62. Citrus Herb Grilled Salmon Burger

- Difficulty Level: Medium
- Prep Time: 10 minutes
- Cooking Time: 10 minutes
- Total Time: 20 minutes
- Temperature: Medium-High Heat
- Cooking Type: Griddling, Searing
- Servings: 1 person

Ingredients:
- 4 oz salmon fillet, skin removed
- 1 tbsp chopped fresh dill
- 1 tsp lemon zest
- 1 hamburger bun
- 1 tbsp olive oil
- Salt and pepper to taste
- 1 tbsp dill yogurt sauce (Greek yogurt mixed with chopped dill and lemon juice)
- 1 slice tomato
- Fresh spinach leaves

Nutritional value (per serving):
Calories: 400 | Protein: 30g | Carbohydrates: 25g | Fats: 20g | Fiber: 2g

Instructions:
1. Preheat the Griddle: Set your gas griddle to medium-high heat.
2. Prepare the Patty: Chop the salmon fillet finely and mix with chopped dill, lemon zest, salt, and pepper. Form into a patty.
3. Cook the Patty: Drizzle olive oil on the griddle. Place the salmon patty on the griddle and cook for about 4-5 minutes per side until browned and cooked through.
4. Toast the Bun: Place the hamburger bun on the griddle, cut side down, and toast for about 1 minute.
5. Assemble the Burger: Spread the dill yogurt sauce on the bottom bun. Add the patty. Top with a slice of tomato and fresh spinach leaves. Place the top bun on.
6. Serve immediately.

Serving Suggestions:
1. Serve with a side of roasted asparagus or a small green salad.

HOT DOG RECIPES

63. Classic New York Style Hot Dog

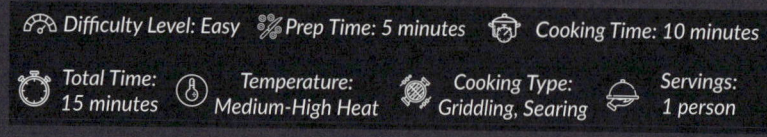

- Difficulty Level: Easy
- Prep Time: 5 minutes
- Cooking Time: 10 minutes
- Total Time: 15 minutes
- Temperature: Medium-High Heat
- Cooking Type: Griddling, Searing
- Servings: 1 person

Ingredients:
- 1 hot dog
- 1 hot dog bun
- 1 tbsp olive oil
- 1 tbsp sauerkraut
- 1 tbsp diced onions
- 1 tbsp yellow mustard
- Salt and pepper to taste

Nutritional value *(per serving)*:

Calories: 300 | Protein: 12g
Carbohydrates: 28g | Fats: 16g | Fiber: 2g

Instructions:
1. Preheat the Griddle: Set your gas griddle to medium-high heat.
2. Cook the Hot Dog: Drizzle olive oil on the griddle. Place the hot dog on the griddle and cook for about 5-7 minutes, turning occasionally until heated through and slightly charred.
3. Toast the Bun: Place the hot dog bun on the griddle, cut side down, and toast for about 1 minute until lightly browned.
4. Assemble the Hot Dog: Place the cooked hot dog in the toasted bun. Top with sauerkraut, diced onions, and yellow mustard.
5. Serve immediately.

Serving Suggestions:
1. Serve with a side of potato chips or a small salad.

64. Chicago-Style Loaded Hot Dog

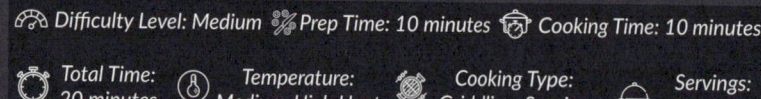

- Difficulty Level: Medium
- Prep Time: 10 minutes
- Cooking Time: 10 minutes
- Total Time: 20 minutes
- Temperature: Medium-High Heat
- Cooking Type: Griddling, Searing
- Servings: 1 person

Ingredients:
- 1 hot dog
- 1 poppy seed hot dog bun
- 1 tbsp olive oil
- 1 pickle spear
- 2 tomato slices
- 1 tbsp diced onions
- 1 tbsp sweet pickle relish
- 2 sport peppers
- 1 dash of celery salt
- 1 tbsp yellow mustard

Nutritional value *(per serving)*:

Calories: 350 | Protein: 14g
Carbohydrates: 32g | Fats: 18g | Fiber: 3g

Instructions:
1. Preheat the Griddle: Set your gas griddle to medium-high heat.
2. Cook the Hot Dog: Drizzle olive oil on the griddle. Place the hot dog on the griddle and cook for about 5-7 minutes, turning occasionally until heated through and slightly charred.
3. Toast the Bun: Place the poppy seed hot dog bun on the griddle, cut side down, and toast for about 1 minute until lightly browned.
4. Assemble the Hot Dog: Place the cooked hot dog in the toasted bun. Add the pickle spear, tomato slices, diced onions, sweet pickle relish, and sport peppers. Sprinkle with celery salt and top with yellow mustard.
5. Serve immediately.

Serving Suggestions:
1. Serve with a side of coleslaw or French fries.

65. Bacon-Wrapped Jalapeño Cheese Dog

- Difficulty Level: Medium
- Prep Time: 10 minutes
- Cooking Time: 10 minutes
- Total Time: 20 minutes
- Temperature: Medium-High Heat
- Cooking Type: Griddling, Searing
- Servings: 1 person

Ingredients:
- 1 hot dog
- 1 slice bacon
- 1 jalapeño, sliced
- 1 slice of cheddar cheese
- 1 hot dog bun
- 1 tbsp olive oil

Nutritional value (per serving):
Calories: 450 | Protein: 20g
Carbohydrates: 30g | Fats: 30g | Fiber: 2g

Instructions:
1. Preheat the Griddle: Set your gas griddle to medium-high heat.
2. Wrap the Hot Dog: Wrap the slice of bacon around the hot dog, securing it with toothpicks if necessary.
3. Cook the Hot Dog: Drizzle olive oil on the griddle. Place the bacon-wrapped hot dog on the griddle and cook for about 7-10 minutes, occasionally turning until the bacon is crispy and the hot dog is heated.
4. Toast the Bun: Place the hot dog bun on the griddle, cut side down, and toast for about 1 minute until lightly browned.
5. Add Cheese and Jalapeños: Place the slice of cheddar cheese on the bun and add the sliced jalapeños. Add the cooked bacon-wrapped hot dog.
6. Serve immediately.

Serving Suggestions:
1. Serve with a side of tortilla chips and salsa.

66. Chili Cheese Dog with Onions

- Difficulty Level: Medium
- Prep Time: 10 minutes
- Cooking Time: 10 minutes
- Total Time: 20 minutes
- Temperature: Medium-High Heat
- Cooking Type: Griddling, Searing, Sautéing
- Servings: 1 person

Ingredients:
- 1 hot dog
- 1 hot dog bun
- 1 tbsp olive oil
- 1/4 cup chili
- 1/4 cup shredded cheddar cheese
- 1 tbsp diced onions

Nutritional value (per serving):
Calories: 500 | Protein: 22g
Carbohydrates: 35g | Fats: 30g | Fiber: 3g

Instructions:
1. Preheat the Griddle: Set your gas griddle to medium-high heat.
2. Cook the Hot Dog: Drizzle olive oil on the griddle. Place the hot dog on the griddle and cook for about 5-7 minutes, turning occasionally until heated through and slightly charred.
3. Heat the Chili: Heat the chili in a small saucepan on the griddle, stirring occasionally, until hot.
4. Toast the Bun: Place the hot dog bun on the griddle, cut side down, and toast for about 1 minute until lightly browned.
5. Assemble the Hot Dog: Place the cooked hot dog in the toasted bun. Top with hot chili, shredded cheddar cheese, and diced onions.
6. Serve immediately.

Serving Suggestions:
1. Serve with a side of coleslaw or potato chips.

67. BBQ Pulled Pork Hot Dog

- Difficulty Level: Medium
- Prep Time: 15 minutes
- Cooking Time: 10 minutes
- Total Time: 25 minutes
- Temperature: Medium-High Heat
- Cooking Type: Griddling, Searing, Sautéing
- Servings: 1 person

Ingredients:
- 1 hot dog
- 1 hot dog bun
- 1 tbsp olive oil
- 1/4 cup pulled pork
- 2 tbsp BBQ sauce
- 1 tbsp coleslaw

Nutritional value (per serving)
Calories: 600 | Protein: 28g | Carbohydrates: 40g | Fats: 35g | Fiber: 2g

Instructions:
1. **Preheat the Griddle:** Set your gas griddle to medium-high heat.
2. **Cook the Hot Dog:** Drizzle olive oil on the griddle. Place the hot dog on the griddle and cook for about 5-7 minutes, turning occasionally until heated through and slightly charred.
3. **Heat the Pulled Pork:** On the griddle, heat the pulled pork with BBQ sauce in a small saucepan, stirring occasionally until hot.
4. **Toast the Bun:** Place the hot dog bun on the griddle, cut side down, and toast for about 1 minute until lightly browned.
5. **Assemble the Hot Dog:** Place the cooked hot dog in the toasted bun. Top with BBQ pulled pork and a spoonful of coleslaw.
6. Serve immediately.

Serving Suggestions:
1. Serve with a side of baked beans or corn on the cob.

STEAK RECIPES

68. Garlic Butter Ribeye Steak

- Difficulty Level: Medium
- Prep Time: 10 minutes
- Cooking Time: 10 minutes
- Total Time: 20 minutes
- Temperature: Medium-High Heat
- Cooking Type: Searing
- Servings: 1 person

Ingredients:
- 8 oz ribeye steak
- 2 tbsp unsalted butter
- 2 garlic cloves, minced
- 1 tbsp fresh parsley, chopped
- 1 tbsp olive oil
- Salt and pepper to taste

Nutritional value (per serving)
Calories: 600 | Protein: 35g | Carbohydrates: 2g | Fats: 50g | Fiber: 0g

Internal Temperatures:
Rare: 125°F (51°C)
Medium-Rare: 135°F (57°C)
Medium: 145°F (63°C)
Medium-Well: 150°F (66°C)
Well-Done: 160°F (71°C)

Instructions:
1. **Preheat the Griddle:** Set your gas griddle to medium-high heat.
2. **Season the Steak:** Season both sides of the ribeye steak with salt and pepper.
3. **Cook the Steak:** Drizzle olive oil on the griddle. Place the ribeye steak on the griddle and cook for about 4-5 minutes per side for medium-rare, adjusting time for desired doneness.
4. **Make the Garlic Butter:** While the steak is cooking, melt the butter in a small saucepan on the griddle. Add minced garlic and cook until fragrant, about 1 minute. Stir in chopped parsley.
5. **Baste the Steak:** Spoon the garlic butter over the steak during the last minute of cooking.
6. **Rest and Serve:** Remove the steak from the griddle and let it rest for a few minutes before serving.

Serving Suggestions:
1. Serve with a side of mashed potatoes or steamed vegetables.

69. Chimichurri Flank Steak

Difficulty Level: Medium | **Prep Time:** 15 minutes | **Cooking Time:** 10 minutes
Total Time: 25 minutes | **Temperature:** Medium-High Heat | **Cooking Type:** Searing | **Servings:** 1 person

Ingredients:
- 8 oz flank steak
- 1/4 cup chimichurri sauce (store-bought or home-made)
- 1 tbsp olive oil
- Salt and pepper to taste

Nutritional value (per serving):
Calories: 450 | Protein: 35g
Carbohydrates: 2g | Fats: 35g
Fiber: 1g

Internal Temperatures:
Rare: 125°F (51°C)
Medium-Rare: 135°F (57°C)
Medium: 145°F (63°C)
Medium-Well: 150°F (66°C)
Well-Done: 160°F (71°C)

Instructions:
1. **Marinate the Steak:** Rub the flank steak with chimichurri sauce and let it marinate for at least 1 hour.
2. **Preheat the Griddle:** Set your gas griddle to medium-high heat.
3. **Season and Cook the Steak:** Remove excess chimichurri from the steak, season with salt and pepper, and drizzle olive oil on the griddle. Place the steak on the griddle and cook for about 4-5 minutes per side for medium-rare, adjusting time for desired doneness.
4. **Rest and Serve:** Remove the steak from the griddle and let it rest for a few minutes before slicing it against the grain.
5. **Top with Chimichurri:** Drizzle additional chimichurri sauce over the sliced steak before serving.

Serving Suggestions:
1. Serve with a side of grilled vegetables or a fresh salad.

70. Peppercorn Crusted Strip Steak

Difficulty Level: Medium | **Prep Time:** 10 minutes | **Cooking Time:** 10 minutes
Total Time: 20 minutes | **Temperature:** Medium-High Heat | **Cooking Type:** Searing | **Servings:** 1 person

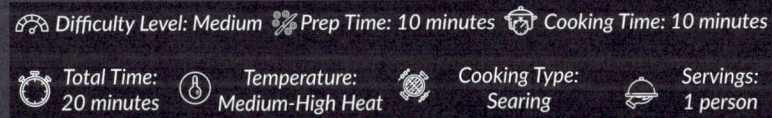

Ingredients:
- 8 oz strip steak
- 1 tbsp black peppercorns, crushed
- 1 tbsp olive oil
- Salt to taste

Nutritional value (per serving):
Calories: 500 | Protein: 35g
Carbohydrates: 2g | Fats: 40g
Fiber: 1g

Internal Temperatures:
Rare: 125°F (51°C)
Medium-Rare: 135°F (57°C)
Medium: 145°F (63°C)
Medium-Well: 150°F (66°C)
Well-Done: 160°F (71°C)

Instructions:
1. **Preheat the Griddle:** Set your gas griddle to medium-high heat.
2. **Season the Steak:** Season the strip steak with salt and press the crushed peppercorns onto both sides of the steak.
3. **Cook the Steak:** Drizzle olive oil on the griddle. Place the steak on the griddle and cook for about 4-5 minutes per side for medium-rare, adjusting time for desired doneness.
4. **Rest and Serve:** Remove the steak from the griddle and let it rest for a few minutes before serving.

Serving Suggestions:
1. Serve with a side of roasted potatoes or a green salad.

71. Classic American Grilled Sirloin

Difficulty Level: Easy | *Prep Time: 5 minutes* | *Cooking Time: 10 minutes* | *Total Time: 15 minutes* | *Temperature: Medium-High Heat* | *Cooking Type: Griddling, Searing* | *Servings: 1 person*

Ingredients:
- 8 oz sirloin steak
- 1 tbsp olive oil
- Salt and pepper to taste

Nutritional value (per serving):
Calories: 450 | Protein: 35g
Carbohydrates: 1g | Fats: 30g
Fiber: 0g

Internal Temperatures:
Rare: 125°F (51°C)
Medium-Rare: 135°F (57°C)
Medium: 145°F (63°C)
Medium-Well: 150°F (66°C)
Well-Done: 160°F (71°C)

Instructions:
1. Preheat the Griddle: Set your gas griddle to medium-high heat.
2. Season the Steak: Season both sides of the sirloin steak with salt and pepper.
3. Cook the Steak: Drizzle olive oil on the griddle. Place the steak on the griddle and cook for about 4-5 minutes per side for medium-rare, adjusting time for desired doneness.
4. Rest and Serve: Remove the steak from the griddle and let it rest for a few minutes before serving.

Serving Suggestions:
1. Serve with a side of French fries or steamed broccoli.

72. Herb-Rubbed T-Bone Steak

Difficulty Level: Medium | *Prep Time: 10 minutes* | *Cooking Time: 12 minutes* | *Total Time: 22 minutes* | *Temperature: Medium-High Heat* | *Cooking Type: Griddling, Searing* | *Servings: 1 person*

Ingredients:
- 12 oz T-bone steak
- 1 tbsp olive oil
- 1 tbsp chopped fresh rosemary
- 1 tbsp chopped fresh thyme
- 2 garlic cloves, minced
- Salt and pepper to taste

Nutritional value (per serving):
Calories: 600 | Protein: 40g
Carbohydrates: 2g | Fats: 45g
Fiber: 1g

Internal Temperatures:
Rare: 125°F (51°C)
Medium-Rare: 135°F (57°C)
Medium: 145°F (63°C)
Medium-Well: 150°F (66°C)
Well-Done: 160°F (71°C)

Instructions:
1. Preheat the Griddle: Set your gas griddle to medium-high heat.
2. Season the Steak: In a small bowl, mix olive oil, rosemary, thyme, minced garlic, salt, and pepper. Rub the mixture onto both sides of the T-bone steak.
3. Cook the Steak: Place the steak on the griddle and cook for about 6-7 minutes per side for medium-rare, adjusting time for desired doneness.
4. Rest and Serve: Remove the steak from the griddle and let it rest for a few minutes before serving.

Serving Suggestions:
1. Serve with a side of mashed potatoes or grilled asparagus.

73. Balsamic Glazed Filet Mignon

Difficulty Level: Medium | Prep Time: 10 minutes | Cooking Time: 10 minutes
Total Time: 20 minutes | Temperature: Medium-High Heat | Cooking Type: Searing | Servings: 1 person

Ingredients:
- 6 oz filet mignon
- 2 tbsp balsamic vinegar
- 1 tbsp olive oil
- Salt and pepper to taste

Nutritional value (per serving):
Calories: 400 | Protein: 30g
Carbohydrates: 8g | Fats: 25g
Fiber: 1g

Internal Temperatures:
Rare: 125°F (51°C)
Medium-Rare: 135°F (57°C)
Medium: 145°F (63°C)
Medium-Well: 150°F (66°C)
Well-Done: 160°F (71°C)

Instructions:
1. Preheat the Griddle: Set your gas griddle to medium-high heat.
2. Season the Steak: Season both sides of the filet mignon with salt and pepper.
3. Cook the Steak: Drizzle olive oil on the griddle. Place the filet mignon on the griddle and cook for 4-5 minutes per side for medium-rare, adjusting time for desired doneness.
4. Add Balsamic Glaze: During the last minute of cooking, drizzle the balsamic vinegar over the steak.
5. Rest and Serve: Remove the steak from the griddle and let it rest for a few minutes before serving.

Serving Suggestions:
1. Serve with a side of roasted Brussels sprouts or a fresh salad.

74. Southwest Spiced Hanger Steak

Difficulty Level: Medium | Prep Time: 10 minutes | Cooking Time: 10 minutes
Total Time: 20 minutes | Temperature: Medium-High Heat | Cooking Type: Searing | Servings: 1 person

Ingredients:
- 8 oz hanger steak
- 1 tbsp olive oil
- 1 tbsp chili powder
- 1 tsp cumin
- 1 tsp paprika
- 1 garlic clove, minced
- Salt and pepper to taste

Nutritional value (per serving):
Calories: 450 | Protein: 35g
Carbohydrates: 3g | Fats: 30g
Fiber: 1g

Internal Temperatures:
Rare: 125°F (51°C)
Medium-Rare: 135°F (57°C)
Medium: 145°F (63°C)
Medium-Well: 150°F (66°C)
Well-Done: 160°F (71°C)

Instructions:
1. Marinate the Steak: In a small bowl, mix olive oil, chili powder, cumin, paprika, minced garlic, salt, and pepper. Rub the mixture onto the hanger steak and let it marinate for at least 1 hour.
2. Preheat the Griddle: Set your gas griddle to medium-high heat.
3. Cook the Steak: Place the steak on the griddle and cook for about 5-6 minutes per side for medium-rare, adjusting time for desired doneness.
4. Rest and Serve: Remove the steak from the griddle and let it rest for a few minutes before slicing it against the grain.

Serving Suggestions:
1. Serve with a side of black beans and rice or a corn salad.

75. Coffee Rubbed Sirloin Steak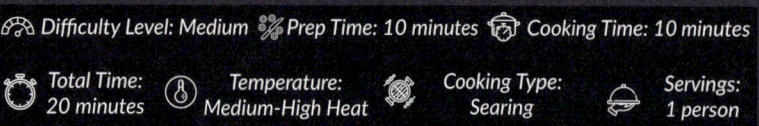

Difficulty Level: Medium **Prep Time:** 10 minutes **Cooking Time:** 10 minutes
Total Time: 20 minutes **Temperature:** Medium-High Heat **Cooking Type:** Searing **Servings:** 1 person

Ingredients:
- 8 oz sirloin steak
- 1 tbsp finely ground coffee
- 1 tsp brown sugar
- 1 tsp smoked paprika
- 1 tbsp olive oil
- Salt and pepper to taste

Nutritional value (per serving):
Calories: 450 | Protein: 35g
Carbohydrates: 3g | Fats: 30g
Fiber: 1g

Instructions:
1. Preheat the Griddle: Set your gas griddle to medium-high heat.
2. Prepare the Rub: In a small bowl, mix ground coffee, brown sugar, smoked paprika, salt, and pepper. Rub the mixture onto both sides of the sirloin steak.
3. Cook the Steak: Drizzle olive oil on the griddle. Place the steak on the griddle and cook for about 4-5 minutes per side for medium-rare, adjusting time for desired doneness.
4. Rest and Serve: Remove the steak from the griddle and let it rest for a few minutes before serving.

Serving Suggestions:
1. Serve with a side of roasted sweet potatoes or a fresh green salad.

Internal Temperatures:
Rare: 125°F (51°C)
Medium-Rare: 135°F (57°C)
Medium: 145°F (63°C)
Medium-Well: 150°F (66°C)
Well-Done: 160°F (71°C)

76. Blue Cheese Crusted New York Strip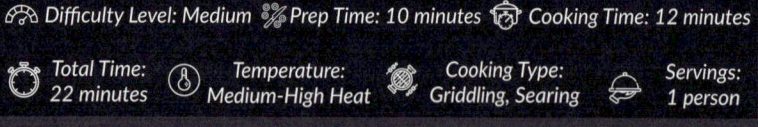

Difficulty Level: Medium **Prep Time:** 10 minutes **Cooking Time:** 12 minutes
Total Time: 22 minutes **Temperature:** Medium-High Heat **Cooking Type:** Griddling, Searing **Servings:** 1 person

Ingredients:
- 8 oz New York strip steak
- 1/4 cup crumbled blue cheese
- 1 tbsp olive oil
- Salt and pepper to taste

Nutritional value (per serving):
Calories: 500 | Protein: 35g
Carbohydrates: 4g | Fats: 35g
Fiber: 1g

Instructions:
1. Preheat the Griddle: Set your gas griddle to medium-high heat.
2. Season the Steak: Season both sides of the New York strip steak with salt and pepper.
3. Cook the Steak: Drizzle olive oil on the griddle. Place the steak on the griddle and cook for 5-6 minutes per side for medium-rare, adjusting time for desired doneness.
4. Add Blue Cheese: During the last minute of cooking, sprinkle the crumbled blue cheese over the steak.
5. Rest and Serve: Remove the steak from the griddle and let it rest for a few minutes before serving.

Serving Suggestions:
1. Serve with a side of roasted potatoes or a green salad.

Internal Temperatures:
Rare: 125°F (51°C)
Medium-Rare: 135°F (57°C)
Medium: 145°F (63°C)
Medium-Well: 150°F (66°C)
Well-Done: 160°F (71°C)

77. Teriyaki Glazed Flat Iron Steak

- Difficulty Level: Medium
- Prep Time: 15 minutes
- Cooking Time: 10 minutes
- Total Time: 25 minutes
- Temperature: Medium-High Heat
- Cooking Type: Searing
- Servings: 1 person

Ingredients:
- 8 oz flat iron steak
- 1/4 cup teriyaki sauce (store-bought or homemade)
- 1 tbsp olive oil
- Salt and pepper to taste

Instructions:
1. Marinate the Steak: Rub the flat iron steak with teriyaki sauce and let it marinate for at least 1 hour.
2. Preheat the Griddle: Set your gas griddle to medium-high heat.
3. Season and Cook the Steak: Remove excess teriyaki sauce from the steak, season with salt and pepper, and drizzle olive oil on the griddle. Place the steak on the griddle and cook for 5-6 minutes per side for medium-rare, adjusting time for desired doneness.
4. Rest and Serve: Remove the steak from the griddle and let it rest for a few minutes before slicing it against the grain.

Serving Suggestions:
1. Serve with a side of steamed rice or stir-fried vegetables.

Nutritional value (per serving):
Calories: 450 | Protein: 35g
Carbohydrates: 10g | Fats: 30g | Fiber: 1g

Internal Temperatures:
Rare: 125°F (51°C)
Medium-Rare: 135°F (57°C)
Medium: 145°F (63°C)
Medium-Well: 150°F (66°C)
Well-Done: 160°F (71°C)

FISH AND SEAFOOD RECIPES

78. Lemon Garlic Grilled Shrimp

- Difficulty Level: Easy
- Prep Time: 10 minutes
- Cooking Time: 5 minutes
- Total Time: 15 minutes
- Temperature: Medium-High Heat
- Cooking Type: Griddling, Searing
- Servings: 1 person

Ingredients:
- 8 oz large shrimp, peeled and deveined
- 2 tbsp olive oil
- 2 garlic cloves, minced
- 1 tbsp lemon juice
- 1 tsp lemon zest
- Salt and pepper to taste
- Fresh parsley, chopped, for garnish

Instructions:
1. Preheat the Griddle: Set your gas griddle to medium-high heat.
2. Prepare the Shrimp: In a bowl, mix olive oil, minced garlic, lemon juice, lemon zest, salt, and pepper. Add shrimp and toss to coat.
3. Cook the Shrimp: Place the shrimp on the griddle and cook for 2-3 minutes per side until they turn pink and opaque.
4. Serve: Garnish with chopped parsley and serve immediately.

Serving Suggestions:
1. Serve with a side of steamed rice or a fresh green salad.

Nutritional value (per serving):
Calories: 200 | Protein: 25g
Carbohydrates: 3g | Fats: 9g
Fiber: 0g

79. Honey Soy Glazed Salmon

Difficulty Level: Medium | **Prep Time:** 10 minutes | **Cooking Time:** 10 minutes
Total Time: 20 minutes | **Temperature:** Medium Heat | **Cooking Type:** Searing, Sautéing | **Servings:** 1 person

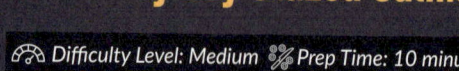

Ingredients:
- 6 oz salmon fillet
- 2 tbsp soy sauce
- 1 tbsp honey
- 1 garlic clove, minced
- 1 tsp grated ginger
- 1 tbsp olive oil
- Sesame seeds, for garnish
- Green onions, sliced, for garnish

Instructions:
1. Preheat the Griddle: Set your gas griddle to medium heat.
2. Prepare the Glaze: In a small bowl, mix soy sauce, honey, minced garlic, and grated ginger.
3. Cook the Salmon: Drizzle olive oil on the griddle. Place the salmon fillet on the griddle, skin side down, and cook for 4-5 minutes. Flip the salmon and cook for another 3-4 minutes, brushing with the honey soy glaze in the last minute of cooking.
4. Serve: Garnish with sesame seeds and sliced green onions.

Nutritional value *(per serving)*:
Calories: 350 | Protein: 30g
Carbohydrates: 20g | Fats: 18g | Fiber: 0g

Serving Suggestions:
1. Serve with a side of steamed rice or sautéed vegetables.

80. Garlic Butter Scallops

Difficulty Level: Medium | **Prep Time:** 10 minutes | **Cooking Time:** 5 minutes
Total Time: 15 minutes | **Temperature:** Medium-High Heat | **Cooking Type:** Searing | **Servings:** 1 person

Ingredients:
- 8 oz sea scallops
- 2 tbsp butter
- 2 garlic cloves, minced
- 1 tbsp olive oil
- Salt and pepper to taste
- Fresh parsley, chopped, for garnish

Instructions:
1. Preheat the Griddle: Set your gas griddle to medium-high heat.
2. Season the Scallops: Season the scallops with salt and pepper.
3. Cook the Scallops: Drizzle olive oil on the griddle. Place the scallops on the griddle and cook for 2-3 minutes per side until golden brown and cooked through.
4. Add Garlic Butter: In the last minute of cooking, add butter and minced garlic to the griddle. Spoon the garlic butter over the scallops.
5. Serve: Garnish with chopped parsley and serve immediately.

Nutritional value *(per serving)*:
Calories: 250 | Protein: 20g
Carbohydrates: 2g | Fats: 18g | Fiber: 0g

Serving Suggestions:
1. Serve with a side of garlic mashed potatoes or a fresh green salad.

81. Teriyaki Mahi-Mahi with Pineapple Salsa

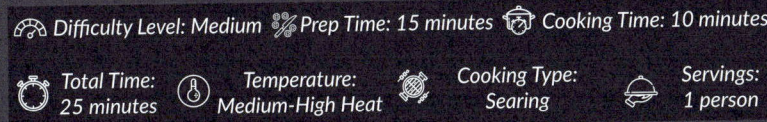

Difficulty Level: Medium | Prep Time: 15 minutes | Cooking Time: 10 minutes
Total Time: 25 minutes | Temperature: Medium-High Heat | Cooking Type: Searing | Servings: 1 person

Ingredients:
- 6 oz mahi-mahi fillet
- 2 tbsp teriyaki sauce
- 1 tbsp olive oil
- For the Pineapple Salsa:
- 1/2 cup diced fresh pineapple
- 1/4 cup diced red onion
- 1/4 cup diced red bell pepper
- 1 tbsp chopped fresh cilantro
- 1 tbsp lime juice
- Salt and pepper to taste

Instructions:
1. Marinate the Mahi-Mahi: Marinate the mahi-mahi fillet in teriyaki sauce for at least 30 minutes.
2. Preheat the Griddle: Set your gas griddle to medium-high heat.
3. Cook the Mahi-Mahi: Drizzle olive oil on the griddle. Place the mahi-mahi fillet on the griddle and cook for 4-5 minutes per side until cooked through.
4. Prepare the Salsa: In a bowl, combine diced pineapple, red onion, red bell pepper, cilantro, lime juice, salt, and pepper.
5. Serve: Top the cooked mahi-mahi with pineapple salsa and serve immediately.

Serving Suggestions:
1. Serve with a side of steamed rice or a green salad.

Nutritional value (per serving):
Calories: 350 | Protein: 28g | Carbohydrates: 20g | Fats: 15g | Fiber: 2g

---

82. Spicy Grilled Swordfish Steaks

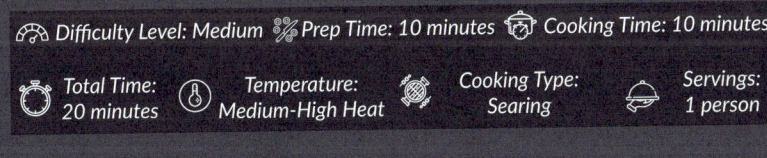

Difficulty Level: Medium | Prep Time: 10 minutes | Cooking Time: 10 minutes
Total Time: 20 minutes | Temperature: Medium-High Heat | Cooking Type: Searing | Servings: 1 person

Ingredients:
- 6 oz swordfish steak
- 2 tbsp olive oil
- 1 garlic clove, minced
- 1 tsp red pepper flakes
- 1 tsp smoked paprika
- Salt and pepper to taste

Instructions:
1. Preheat the Griddle: Set your gas griddle to medium-high heat.
2. Season the Swordfish: In a bowl, mix olive oil, minced garlic, red pepper flakes, smoked paprika, salt, and pepper. Rub the mixture onto both sides of the swordfish steak.
3. Cook the Swordfish: Place the swordfish steak on the griddle and cook for about 4-5 minutes per side until cooked through.
4. Serve immediately.

Serving Suggestions:
1. Serve with a side of grilled vegetables or a quinoa salad.

Nutritional value (per serving):
Calories: 400 | Protein: 35g | Carbohydrates: 3g | Fats: 27g | Fiber: 1g

83. Citrus Herb Grilled Tilapia

Ingredients:
- 6 oz tilapia fillet
- 2 tbsp olive oil
- 1 tsp lemon zest
- 1 tbsp lemon juice
- 1 garlic clove, minced
- 1 tbsp chopped fresh dill
- Salt and pepper to taste

Nutritional value (per serving):
Calories: 250 | Protein: 30g
Carbohydrates: 4g | Fats: 12g
Fiber: 1g

Instructions:
1. Preheat the Griddle: Set your gas griddle to medium-high heat.
2. Season the Tilapia: In a bowl, mix olive oil, lemon zest, lemon juice, minced garlic, chopped dill, salt, and pepper. Rub the mixture onto both sides of the tilapia fillet.
3. Cook the Tilapia: Place the tilapia fillet on the griddle and cook for 4-5 minutes per side until cooked through.
4. Serve immediately.

Serving Suggestions:
1. Serve with a side of roasted vegetables or a fresh green salad.

84. Dill and Lemon Salmon Fillets

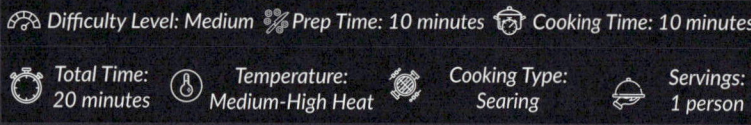

Ingredients:
- 6 oz salmon fillet
- 2 tbsp olive oil
- 1 tbsp lemon juice
- 1 tsp lemon zest
- 1 tbsp chopped fresh dill
- Salt and pepper to taste

Nutritional value (per serving):
Calories: 350 | Protein: 30g
Carbohydrates: 5g | Fats: 20g
Fiber: 1g

Instructions:
1. Preheat the Griddle: Set your gas griddle to medium-high heat.
2. Season the Salmon: In a bowl, mix olive oil, lemon juice, lemon zest, chopped dill, salt, and pepper. Rub the mixture onto both sides of the salmon fillet.
3. Cook the Salmon: Place the salmon fillet on the griddle, skin side down, and cook for about 4-5 minutes. Flip the salmon and cook for another 3-4 minutes until cooked.
4. Serve immediately.

Serving Suggestions:
1. Serve with a side of steamed asparagus or a fresh green salad.

85. Maple Mustard Glazed Salmon

- Difficulty Level: Medium
- Prep Time: 10 minutes
- Cooking Time: 10 minutes
- Total Time: 20 minutes
- Temperature: Medium-High Heat
- Cooking Type: Searing
- Servings: 1 person

Ingredients:
- 6 oz salmon fillet
- 2 tbsp maple syrup
- 1 tbsp Dijon mustard
- 1 tbsp olive oil
- Salt and pepper to taste

Nutritional value (per serving):
Calories: 350 | Protein: 30g Carbohydrates: 10g | Fats: 18g | Fiber: 1g

Instructions:
1. Preheat the Griddle: Set your gas griddle to medium-high heat.
2. Prepare the Glaze: Mix maple syrup and Dijon mustard in a small bowl.
3. Season the Salmon: Season the salmon fillet with salt and pepper.
4. Cook the Salmon: Drizzle olive oil on the griddle. Place the salmon fillet on the griddle, skin side down, and cook for 4-5 minutes. Flip the salmon and cook for another 3-4 minutes, brushing with the maple mustard glaze in the last minute of cooking.
5. Serve immediately.

Serving Suggestions:
1. Serve with a side of roasted Brussels sprouts or a fresh green salad.

SALAD RECIPES

86. Grilled Romaine Caesar Salad

- Difficulty Level: Easy
- Prep Time: 10 minutes
- Cooking Time: 5 minutes
- Total Time: 15 minutes
- Temperature: Medium-High Heat
- Cooking Type: Griddling, Searing
- Servings: 1 person

Ingredients:
- 1 romaine heart, halved lengthwise
- 1 tbsp olive oil
- Salt and pepper to taste
- 2 tbsp Caesar dressing
- 1 tbsp grated Parmesan cheese
- 1/4 cup croutons

Nutritional value (per serving):
Calories: 250 | Protein: 8g Carbohydrates: 15g | Fats: 18g | Fiber: 5g

Instructions:
1. Preheat the Griddle: Set your gas griddle to medium-high heat.
2. Prepare the Romaine: Brush the cut sides of the romaine heart with olive oil and season with salt and pepper.
3. Grill the Romaine: Place the romaine halves cut side down on the griddle and cook for 2-3 minutes until charred and slightly wilted.
4. Assemble the Salad: Place the grilled romaine on a plate. Drizzle with Caesar dressing, sprinkle with grated Parmesan cheese and top with croutons.
5. Serve immediately.

Serving Suggestions:
1. Serve with a side of grilled chicken or shrimp.

87. Mediterranean Quinoa Salad with Feta and Olives

- Difficulty Level: Easy
- Prep Time: 15 minutes
- Cooking Time: 0 minutes
- Total Time: 15 minutes
- Servings: 1 person

Ingredients:

- 1 cup cooked quinoa
- 1/4 cup diced cucumber
- 1/4 cup cherry tomatoes, halved
- 1/4 cup sliced Kalamata olives
- 1/4 cup crumbled feta cheese
- 1 tbsp chopped fresh parsley
- 1 tbsp chopped fresh mint
- 2 tbsp olive oil
- 1 tbsp lemon juice
- Salt and pepper to taste

Instructions:

1. Prepare the Salad: In a large bowl, combine cooked quinoa, diced cucumber, cherry tomatoes, sliced olives, crumbled feta cheese, chopped parsley, and chopped mint.
2. Make the Dressing: In a small bowl, whisk together olive oil, lemon juice, salt, and pepper.
3. Dress the Salad: Pour the dressing over the quinoa salad and toss to combine.
4. Serve immediately or chill before serving.

Serving Suggestions:
1. Serve with pita bread or grilled vegetables.

Nutritional value (per serving):

Calories: 300 | Protein: 10g | Carbohydrates: 35g | Fats: 15g | Fiber: 7g

88. Strawberry Spinach Salad with Balsamic Vinaigrette

- Difficulty Level: Easy
- Prep Time: 10 minutes
- Cooking Time: 0 minutes
- Total Time: 10 minutes
- Servings: 1 person

Ingredients:

- 2 cups fresh baby spinach
- 1/2 cup sliced strawberries
- 1/4 cup crumbled goat cheese
- 2 tbsp sliced almonds
- 2 tbsp balsamic vinaigrette

Instructions:

1. Prepare the Salad: In a large bowl, combine baby spinach, sliced strawberries, crumbled goat cheese, and sliced almonds.
2. Dress the Salad: Drizzle with balsamic vinaigrette and toss to combine.
3. Serve immediately.

Serving Suggestions:
1. Serve with a side of grilled chicken or shrimp.

Nutritional value (per serving):

Calories: 200 | Protein: 5g | Carbohydrates: 20g | Fats: 12g | Fiber: 5g

89. Avocado and Tomato Salad with Lime Dressing

- Difficulty Level: Easy
- Prep Time: 10 minutes
- Cooking Time: 0 minutes
- Total Time: 10 minutes
- Servings: 1 person

Ingredients:
- 1 avocado, diced
- 1 cup cherry tomatoes, halved
- 1/4 cup diced red onion
- 1 tbsp chopped fresh cilantro
- 1 tbsp lime juice
- 1 tbsp olive oil
- Salt and pepper to taste

Instructions:
1. Prepare the Salad: In a large bowl, combine diced avocado, cherry tomatoes, diced red onion, and chopped cilantro.
2. Make the Dressing: In a small bowl, whisk together lime juice, olive oil, salt, and pepper.
3. Dress the Salad: Pour the dressing over the salad and toss to combine.
4. Serve immediately or chill before serving.

Serving Suggestions:
1. Serve with tortilla chips or as a side to grilled fish.

Nutritional value (per serving):
Calories: 250 | Protein: 3g | Carbohydrates: 15g | Fats: 22g | Fiber: 8g

90. Grilled Chicken Cobb Salad

- Difficulty Level: Medium
- Prep Time: 15 minutes
- Cooking Time: 10 minutes
- Total Time: 25 minutes
- Temperature: Medium-High Heat
- Cooking Type: Griddling, Searing
- Servings: 1 person

Ingredients:
- 1 chicken breast
- 1 tbsp olive oil
- Salt and pepper to taste
- 2 cups mixed greens
- 1 hard-boiled egg, sliced
- 1/4 cup cherry tomatoes, halved
- 1/4 cup diced cucumber
- 1/4 avocado, sliced
- 2 tbsp crumbled blue cheese
- 2 tbsp ranch dressing

Instructions:
1. Preheat the Griddle: Set your gas griddle to medium-high heat.
2. Cook the Chicken: Drizzle olive oil on the griddle. Season the chicken breast with salt and pepper and place it on the griddle. Cook for about 5-6 minutes per side until the chicken is cooked and reaches an internal temperature of 165°F (74°C). Remove and let it rest before slicing.
3. Prepare the Salad: In a large bowl, combine mixed greens, sliced hard-boiled egg, cherry tomatoes, diced cucumber, sliced avocado, and crumbled blue cheese.
4. Add the Chicken: Slice the cooked chicken breast and add it to the salad.
5. Dress the Salad: Drizzle with ranch dressing and toss to combine.
6. Serve immediately.

Serving Suggestions:
1. Serve with a slice of crusty bread or a light soup.

Nutritional value (per serving):
Calories: 450 | Protein: 35g | Carbohydrates: 20g | Fats: 25g | Fiber: 6g

RECIPES FOR SPECIAL OCCASIONS

91. Garlic Butter Lobster Tails

Difficulty Level: Medium Prep Time: 10 minutes Cooking Time: 10 minutes
Total Time: 20 minutes Temperature: Medium-High Heat Cooking Type: Griddling, Searing Servings: 1 person

Ingredients:
- 1 lobster tail
- 2 tbsp unsalted butter
- 2 garlic cloves, minced
- 1 tbsp lemon juice
- Salt and pepper to taste
- Fresh parsley, chopped, for garnish

Nutritional value (per serving):
Calories: 350 | Protein: 25g
Carbohydrates: 2g | Fats: 27g
Fiber: 0g

Instructions:
1. Preheat the Griddle: Set your gas griddle to medium-high heat.
2. Prepare the Lobster Tail: Using kitchen shears, cut down the top shell of the lobster tail to expose the meat. Gently lift the meat from the shell, keeping it attached at the base.
3. Cook the Lobster Tail: Place the lobster tail on the griddle, with the shell side down. Cook for 5-7 minutes until the meat is opaque and cooked through.
4. Make the Garlic Butter: Melt the butter in a small saucepan on the griddle. Add minced garlic and cook until fragrant, about 1 minute. Stir in lemon juice, salt, and pepper.
5. Baste the Lobster Tail: Spoon the garlic butter over the lobster tail during the last minute of cooking.
6. Serve: Garnish with chopped parsley and serve immediately.

Serving Suggestions:
1. Serve with a side of garlic mashed potatoes or steamed vegetables.

92. Herb-Crusted Rack of Lamb

Difficulty Level: Medium Prep Time: 15 minutes Cooking Time: 20 minutes
Total Time: 35 minutes Temperature: Medium-High Heat Cooking Type: Searing, Indirect Cooking Servings: 1 person

Ingredients:
- 4 ribs from a rack of lamb
- 2 tbsp olive oil
- 2 garlic cloves, minced
- 1 tbsp chopped fresh rosemary
- 1 tbsp chopped fresh thyme
- Salt and pepper to taste

Nutritional value (per serving):
Calories: 600 | Protein: 45g
Carbohydrates: 3g | Fats: 45g
Fiber: 1g

Instructions:
1. Preheat the Griddle: Set your gas griddle to medium-high heat.
2. Prepare the Lamb: In a small bowl, mix olive oil, minced garlic, chopped rosemary, chopped thyme, salt, and pepper. Rub the mixture onto the lamb.
3. Sear the Lamb: Place the lamb on the griddle and sear for 2-3 minutes per side until browned.
4. Cook the Lamb: Reduce the heat to medium. Cook the lamb for an additional 10-15 minutes, turning occasionally, until it reaches an internal temperature of 135°F (57°C) for medium-rare.
5. Rest and Serve: Remove the lamb from the griddle and let it rest for a few minutes before slicing.

Serving Suggestions:
1. Serve with a side of roasted potatoes or a fresh green salad.

93. Tropical Mango and Avocado Ceviche with Fish

- Difficulty Level: Easy
- Prep Time: 15 minutes
- Cooking Time: 0 minutes
- Total Time: 15 minutes
- Servings: 1 person

Ingredients:
- 1/2 cup diced mango
- 1/2 avocado, diced
- 1/4 cup diced red onion
- 1/4 cup diced red bell pepper
- 1/4 cup chopped fresh cilantro
- 1/4 pound fresh white fish (such as tilapia, sea bass, or snapper), cut into small cubes
- 1 tbsp lime juice
- 1 tbsp lemon juice
- Salt and pepper to taste

Instructions:
1. Prepare the Fish: Place the fish cubes in a bowl and add lime juice and lemon juice. Mix gently to combine, then cover and refrigerate for 15 minutes to allow the fish to "cook" in the citrus juices.
2. Prepare the Ceviche: In a large bowl, combine diced mango, avocado, red onion, red bell pepper, and chopped cilantro.
3. Make the Dressing: In a small bowl, mix additional lime juice, lemon juice, salt, and pepper.
4. Dress the Ceviche: Drain the marinated fish, then add it to the mango and avocado mixture. Pour the dressing over the ceviche and toss gently to combine.
5. Serve: Chill for at least 30 minutes before serving.

Serving Suggestions:
1. Serve with tortilla chips or as a side to grilled seafood

Nutritional value (per serving):
Calories: 300 | Protein: 15g | Carbohydrates: 30g | Fats: 15g | Fiber: 8g

94. Balsamic Glazed Duck Breast

- Difficulty Level: Medium
- Prep Time: 10 minutes
- Cooking Time: 15 minutes
- Total Time: 25 minutes
- Temperature: Medium-High Heat
- Cooking Type: Searing, Sautéing
- Servings: 1 person

Ingredients:
- 1 duck breast
- 2 tbsp balsamic vinegar
- 1 tbsp honey
- 1 tbsp olive oil
- Salt and pepper to taste

Instructions:
1. Preheat the Griddle: Set your gas griddle to medium-high heat.
2. Prepare the Duck Breast: Score the skin of the duck breast in a crosshatch pattern. Season with salt and pepper.
3. Sear the Duck Breast: Place the duck breast skin side down on the griddle and cook for about 6-7 minutes until the skin is crispy. Flip and cook for an additional 5-6 minutes until the internal temperature reaches 135°F (57°C) for medium-rare.
4. Make the Glaze: Mix balsamic vinegar and honey in a small saucepan on the griddle. Cook until the mixture reduces and thickens.
5. Glaze the Duck Breast: Brush the balsamic glaze over the duck breast in the last minute of cooking.
6. Rest and Serve: Remove the duck breast from the griddle and let it rest for a few minutes before slicing.

Serving Suggestions:
1. Serve with a side of roasted vegetables or a fresh green salad.

Nutritional value (per serving):
Calories: 450 | Protein: 30g | Carbohydrates: 10g | Fats: 30g | Fiber: 1g

95. Grilled Surf and Turf (Steak and Shrimp)

Difficulty Level: Medium | Prep Time: 10 minutes | Cooking Time: 15 minutes
Total Time: 25 minutes | Temperature: Medium-High Heat | Cooking Type: Griddling, Searing | Servings: 1 person

Ingredients:
- 6 oz steak (ribeye or sirloin)
- 8 large shrimp, peeled and deveined
- 2 tbsp olive oil
- 2 garlic cloves, minced
- 1 tbsp lemon juice
- Salt and pepper to taste
- Fresh parsley, chopped, for garnish

Nutritional value (per serving):
Calories: 500 | Protein: 45g
Carbohydrates: 5g | Fats: 30g
Fiber: 1g

Instructions:
1. Preheat the Griddle: Set your gas griddle to medium-high heat.
2. Season the Steak and Shrimp: Season the steak and shrimp with salt and pepper. Drizzle olive oil over them.
3. Cook the Steak: Place the steak on the griddle and cook for about 4-5 minutes per side for medium-rare, adjusting time for desired doneness. Remove and let it rest.
4. Cook the Shrimp: Place the shrimp on the griddle for the last few minutes of cooking the steak. Cook for 2-3 minutes per side until pink and opaque.
5. Make the Garlic Butter: Melt butter in a small saucepan on the griddle. Add minced garlic and cook until fragrant, about 1 minute. Stir in lemon juice.
6. Serve: Slice the steak and arrange it on a plate with the shrimp. Drizzle with garlic butter and garnish with chopped parsley.

Serving Suggestions:
1. Serve with a side of garlic mashed potatoes or steamed vegetables.

96. Maple Glazed Holiday Ham

Difficulty Level: Medium | Prep Time: 10 minutes | Cooking Time: 30 minutes
Total Time: 40 minutes | Temperature: Medium Heat | Cooking Type: Griddling, Searing | Servings: 1 person

Ingredients:
- 8 oz slice of pre-cooked ham
- 2 tbsp maple syrup
- 1 tbsp Dijon mustard
- 1 tbsp brown sugar
- 1 tbsp olive oil

Nutritional value (per serving):
Calories: 450 | Protein: 30g
Carbohydrates: 25g | Fats: 25g | Fiber: 1g

Instructions:
1. Preheat the Griddle: Set your gas griddle to medium heat.
2. Prepare the Glaze: In a small bowl, mix maple syrup, Dijon mustard, and brown sugar.
3. Cook the Ham: Drizzle olive oil on the griddle. Place the ham slice on the griddle and cook for about 10-15 minutes, turning occasionally and brushing with the maple glaze until heated through and caramelized.
4. Serve immediately.

Serving Suggestions:
1. Serve with a side of roasted sweet potatoes or green beans.

97. Prosciutto-Wrapped Asparagus Bundles

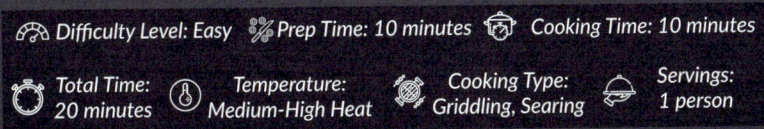

- Difficulty Level: Easy
- Prep Time: 10 minutes
- Cooking Time: 10 minutes
- Total Time: 20 minutes
- Temperature: Medium-High Heat
- Cooking Type: Griddling, Searing
- Servings: 1 person

Ingredients:
- 8 asparagus spears
- 4 slices prosciutto
- 1 tbsp olive oil
- Salt and pepper to taste

Nutritional value (per serving):
Calories: 150 | Protein: 8g
Carbohydrates: 5g | Fats: 10g
Fiber: 2g

Instructions:
1. Preheat the Griddle: Set your gas griddle to medium-high heat.
2. Wrap the Asparagus: Wrap 2 asparagus spears in each slice of prosciutto.
3. Cook the Asparagus Bundles: Drizzle olive oil on the griddle. Place the prosciutto-wrapped asparagus bundles on the griddle and cook for about 5-7 minutes, turning occasionally, until the asparagus is tender and the prosciutto is crispy.
4. Serve: Season with salt and pepper to taste and serve immediately.

Serving Suggestions:
1. Serve with a side of garlic aioli or a fresh green salad.

LOW CALORIES RECIPES

98. Grilled Lemon Herb Chicken Breast

- Difficulty Level: Easy
- Prep Time: 10 minutes
- Cooking Time: 10 minutes
- Total Time: 20 minutes
- Temperature: Medium-High Heat
- Cooking Type: Griddling, Searing
- Servings: 1 person

Ingredients:
- 1 boneless, skinless chicken breast
- 2 tbsp olive oil
- 1 tbsp lemon juice
- 1 tsp lemon zest
- 1 garlic clove, minced
- 1 tsp dried oregano
- 1 tsp dried thyme
- Salt and pepper to taste

Instructions:
1. Marinate the Chicken: In a small bowl, mix olive oil, lemon juice, lemon zest, minced garlic, dried oregano, dried thyme, salt, and pepper. Marinate the chicken breast in the mixture for at least 30 minutes.
2. Preheat the Griddle: Set your gas griddle to medium-high heat.
3. Cook the Chicken: Place the chicken breast on the griddle and cook for about 5-6 minutes per side until the internal temperature reaches 165°F (74°C).
4. Serve immediately.

Serving Suggestions:
1. Serve with a side of steamed broccoli or a mixed green salad.

Nutritional value (per serving):
Calories: 200 | Protein: 30g
Carbohydrates: 3g | Fats: 8g
Fiber: 0g

99. Zesty Shrimp and Veggie Skewers

◐ Difficulty Level: Medium ✂ Prep Time: 15 minutes 🍲 Cooking Time: 10 minutes
⏱ Total Time: 25 minutes 🌡 Temperature: Medium-High Heat 🍳 Cooking Type: Griddling, Searing 🍽 Servings: 1 person

Ingredients:
- 8 large shrimp, peeled and deveined
- 1/2 red bell pepper, cut into chunks
- 1/2 zucchini, sliced
- 1/4 red onion, cut into chunks
- 2 tbsp olive oil
- 1 tbsp lime juice
- 1 tsp chili powder
- Salt and pepper to taste

Instructions:
1. Prepare the Skewers: Thread the shrimp, red bell pepper, zucchini, and red onion onto skewers.
2. Marinate the Skewers: In a small bowl, mix olive oil, lime juice, chili powder, salt, and pepper. Brush the mixture onto the skewers.
3. Preheat the Griddle: Set your gas griddle to medium-high heat.
4. Cook the Skewers: Place the skewers on the griddle and cook for 3-4 minutes per side until the shrimp are pink and opaque and the vegetables are tender.
5. Serve immediately.

Serving Suggestions:
1. Serve with a side of quinoa or a fresh salad.

Nutritional value (per serving):
Calories: 180 | Protein: 20g
Carbohydrates: 8g | Fats: 7g
Fiber: 2g

100. Spicy Cauliflower Steaks

◐ Difficulty Level: Medium ✂ Prep Time: 10 minutes 🍲 Cooking Time: 15 minutes
⏱ Total Time: 25 minutes 🌡 Temperature: Medium-High Heat 🍳 Cooking Type: Griddling, Searing 🍽 Servings: 1 person

Ingredients:
- 1 large cauliflower, cut into 1-inch thick steaks
- 2 tbsp olive oil
- 1 tsp smoked paprika
- 1 tsp garlic powder
- 1/2 tsp cayenne pepper
- Salt and pepper to taste

Instructions:
1. Prepare the Cauliflower: In a small bowl, mix olive oil, smoked paprika, garlic powder, cayenne pepper, salt, and pepper. Brush the mixture onto both sides of the cauliflower steaks.
2. Preheat the Griddle: Set your gas griddle to medium-high heat.
3. Cook the Cauliflower: Place the cauliflower steaks on the griddle and cook for about 7-8 minutes per side until golden brown and tender.
4. Serve immediately.

Serving Suggestions:
1. Serve with a side of mixed greens or roasted chickpeas.

Nutritional value (per serving):
Calories: 150 | Protein: 5g
Carbohydrates: 18g | Fats: 8g
Fiber: 6g

101. Turkey and Veggie Lettuce Wraps

Difficulty Level: Easy | Prep Time: 10 minutes | Cooking Time: 10 minutes
Total Time: 20 minutes | Temperature: Medium Heat | Cooking Type: Sautéing, Griddling | Servings: 1 person

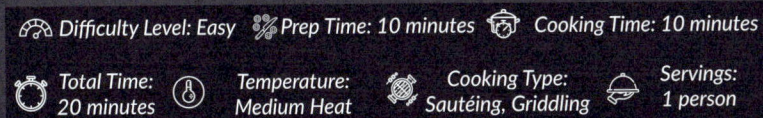

Ingredients:
- 4 oz ground turkey
- 1/2 cup diced bell pepper
- 1/2 cup diced zucchini
- 1/4 cup diced red onion
- 1 tbsp olive oil
- 2 tbsp soy sauce
- 1 tsp garlic powder
- Salt and pepper to taste
- 4 large lettuce leaves (e.g., Romaine or Butterhead)

Instructions:
1. Cook the Turkey and Veggies: Drizzle olive oil on the griddle and set to medium heat. Add ground turkey, bell pepper, zucchini, and red onion. Cook for about 7-8 minutes, stirring occasionally, until the turkey is cooked and the vegetables tender. Add soy sauce, garlic powder, salt, and pepper, and cook for 2 minutes.
2. Assemble the Wraps: Spoon the turkey and veggie mixture onto the center of each lettuce leaf.
3. Serve immediately.

Serving Suggestions:
1. Serve with a side of fresh salsa or guacamole.

Nutritional value (per serving):
Calories: 200 | Protein: 20g
Carbohydrates: 10g | Fats: 10g | Fiber: 3g

102. Blackened Tilapia with Mango Salsa

Difficulty Level: Medium | Prep Time: 10 minutes | Cooking Time: 10 minutes
Total Time: 20 minutes | Temperature: Medium-High Heat | Cooking Type: Searing, Griddling | Servings: 1 person

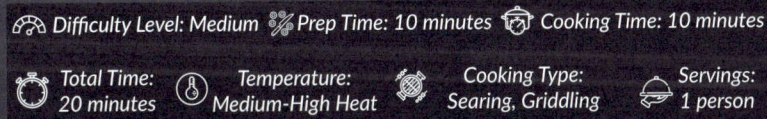

Ingredients:
- 1 tilapia fillet
- 1 tbsp olive oil
- 1 tbsp blackening seasoning
- Salt and pepper to taste

For the Mango Salsa:
- 1/2 cup diced mango
- 1/4 cup diced red bell pepper
- 1/4 cup diced red onion
- 1 tbsp chopped fresh cilantro
- 1 tbsp lime juice
- Salt and pepper to taste

Instructions:
1. Prepare the Salsa: In a bowl, combine diced mango, red bell pepper, red onion, chopped cilantro, lime juice, salt, and pepper. Mix well and set aside.
2. Season the Tilapia: Rub the tilapia fillet with olive oil and blackening seasoning.
3. Preheat the Griddle: Set your gas griddle to medium-high heat.
4. Cook the Tilapia: Place the tilapia fillet on the griddle and cook for 3-4 minutes per side until blackened and cooked through.
5. Serve: Top the tilapia with mango salsa and serve immediately.

Serving Suggestions:
1. Serve with a side of quinoa or a fresh green salad.

Nutritional value (per serving):
Calories: 250 | Protein: 25g
Carbohydrates: 15g | Fats: 10g | Fiber: 3g

103. Grilled Portobello Mushrooms with Balsamic Glaze

- Difficulty Level: Easy
- Prep Time: 10 minutes
- Cooking Time: 10 minutes
- Total Time: 20 minutes
- Temperature: Medium-High Heat
- Cooking Type: Griddling, Searing
- Servings: 1 person

Ingredients:
- 2 large Portobello mushrooms
- 2 tbsp olive oil
- 2 tbsp balsamic vinegar
- 1 garlic clove, minced
- 1 tsp honey
- Salt and pepper to taste

Nutritional value (per serving):
Calories: 150 | Protein: 4g
Carbohydrates: 15g | Fats: 8g
Fiber: 4g

Instructions:
1. Prepare the Mushrooms: Clean the mushrooms and remove the stems. Brush with olive oil and season with salt and pepper.
2. Preheat the Griddle: Set your gas griddle to medium-high heat.
3. Cook the Mushrooms: Place the mushrooms on the griddle, cap side down. Cook for about 5 minutes per side until tender.
4. Make the Balsamic Glaze: In a small saucepan, mix balsamic vinegar, minced garlic, and honey on the griddle. Cook until the mixture reduces and thickens slightly.
5. Serve: Drizzle the balsamic glaze over the grilled mushrooms and serve immediately.

Serving Suggestions:
1. Serve with a side of quinoa or a fresh green salad.

MEXICAN CUISINE RECIPES

104. Beef and Cheese Quesadillas

- Difficulty Level: Easy
- Prep Time: 10 minutes
- Cooking Time: 10 minutes
- Total Time: 20 minutes
- Temperature: Medium Heat
- Cooking Type: Griddling, Searing
- Servings: 1 person

Ingredients:
- 1/4 lb ground beef
- 1/2 cup shredded cheddar cheese
- 1/4 cup diced bell pepper
- 1/4 cup diced onion
- 2 large flour tortillas
- 1 tbsp olive oil
- 1 tsp taco seasoning
- Salt and pepper to taste

Nutritional value (per serving):
Calories: 400 | Protein: 20g
Carbohydrates: 35g | Fats: 20g | Fiber: 4g

Instructions:
1. Cook the Beef: Preheat the griddle to medium heat. Drizzle olive oil and cook the ground beef with diced bell pepper, onion, taco seasoning, salt, and pepper until the meat is browned and cooked. Remove from the griddle and set aside.
2. Assemble the Quesadilla: Place one tortilla on the griddle. Sprinkle half of the shredded cheese, add the cooked beef mixture, and top with the remaining cheese. Place the second tortilla on top.
3. Cook the Quesadilla: Cook for 3-4 minutes per side until the tortillas are golden brown and the cheese is melted.
4. Serve: Slice into wedges and serve immediately.

Serving Suggestions:
1. Serve with sour cream, guacamole, or salsa.

105. Grilled Chicken Tacos with Fresh Pico de Gallo

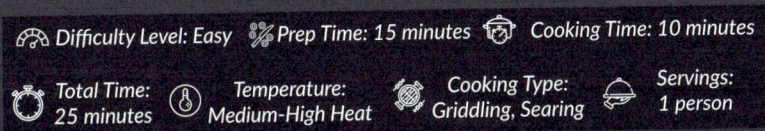

- Difficulty Level: Easy
- Prep Time: 15 minutes
- Cooking Time: 10 minutes
- Total Time: 25 minutes
- Temperature: Medium-High Heat
- Cooking Type: Griddling, Searing
- Servings: 1 person

Ingredients:

For the Chicken:
- 1 boneless, skinless chicken breast
- 1 tbsp olive oil
- 1 tsp chili powder
- 1 tsp cumin
- 1 garlic clove, minced
- Salt and pepper to taste

For the Pico de Gallo:
- 1/2 cup diced tomatoes
- 1/4 cup diced red onion
- 1/4 cup chopped fresh cilantro
- 1 tbsp lime juice
- Salt and pepper to taste
- 2 small corn tortillas
- Lime wedges for serving

Instructions:

1. Marinate the Chicken: In a bowl, mix olive oil, chili powder, cumin, minced garlic, salt, and pepper. Marinate the chicken breast in the mixture for at least 30 minutes.
2. Prepare the Pico de Gallo: In a separate bowl, combine diced tomatoes, red onion, cilantro, lime juice, salt, and pepper. Mix well and set aside.
3. Preheat the Griddle: Set your gas griddle to medium-high heat.
4. Cook the Chicken: Place the chicken breast on the griddle and cook for about 5-6 minutes per side until the internal temperature reaches 165°F (74°C). Remove and let it rest before slicing.
5. Warm the Tortillas: Place the tortillas on the griddle and warm them for about 1 minute per side.
6. Assemble the Tacos: Slice the chicken and place it on the tortillas. Top with fresh pico de gallo.
7. Serve with lime wedges.

Serving Suggestions:
1. Serve with a side of black beans or a fresh salad.

Nutritional value (per serving):

Calories: 300 | Protein: 25g
Carbohydrates: 20g | Fats: 12g | Fiber: 3g

106. Pork Carnitas Tostadas

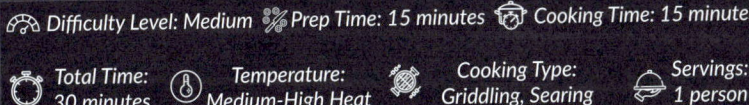

- Difficulty Level: Medium
- Prep Time: 15 minutes
- Cooking Time: 15 minutes
- Total Time: 30 minutes
- Temperature: Medium-High Heat
- Cooking Type: Griddling, Searing
- Servings: 1 person

Ingredients:

- 1/2 lb pork shoulder, cooked and shredded
- 2 tostada shells
- 1/4 cup refried beans
- 1/4 cup shredded lettuce
- 1/4 cup diced tomatoes
- 1/4 cup crumbled queso fresco
- 1 tbsp olive oil
- 1 tsp cumin
- 1 tsp chili powder
- Salt and pepper to taste

Instructions:

1. Prepare the Pork: Preheat the griddle to medium-high heat. Drizzle olive oil and cook the shredded pork with cumin, chili powder, salt, and pepper until crispy.
2. Warm the Tostada Shells: Place the tostada shells on the griddle for about 1 minute per side until crisp.
3. Assemble the Tostadas: Spread refried beans on each tostada shell. Top with crispy pork, shredded lettuce, diced tomatoes, and crumbled queso fresco.
4. Serve immediately.

Serving Suggestions:
1. Serve with a side of Mexican rice or black beans.

Nutritional value (per serving):

Calories: 350 | Protein: 25g
Carbohydrates: 20g | Fats: 18g | Fiber: 3g

107. Shrimp Fajitas with Bell Peppers and Onions

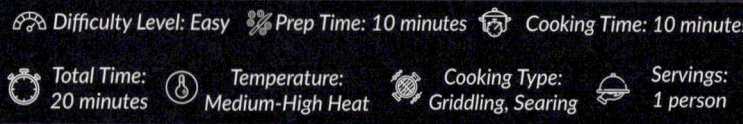

- Difficulty Level: Easy
- Prep Time: 10 minutes
- Cooking Time: 10 minutes
- Total Time: 20 minutes
- Temperature: Medium-High Heat
- Cooking Type: Griddling, Searing
- Servings: 1 person

Ingredients:

- 8 large shrimp, peeled and deveined
- 1/2 cup sliced bell peppers (red, yellow, green)
- 1/4 cup sliced onion
- 2 tbsp olive oil
- 1 tsp fajita seasoning
- Salt and pepper to taste
- 2 small flour tortillas

Instructions:

1. Prepare the Shrimp and Veggies: In a bowl, toss shrimp, bell peppers, and onions with olive oil, fajita seasoning, salt, and pepper.
2. Preheat the Griddle: Set your gas griddle to medium-high heat.
3. Cook the Shrimp and Veggies: Place the shrimp and veggies on the griddle. Cook for 3-4 minutes per side until the shrimp are pink and opaque, and the veggies are tender.
4. Warm the Tortillas: Place the tortillas on the griddle for about 1 minute per side until warm.
5. Assemble the Fajitas: Place the shrimp and veggies on the tortillas.
6. Serve immediately.

Serving Suggestions:
1. Serve with a side of guacamole or salsa.

Nutritional value (per serving):
Calories: 250 | Protein: 20g
Carbohydrates: 20g | Fats: 10g | Fiber: 5g

108. Vegetarian Black Bean and Corn Enchiladas

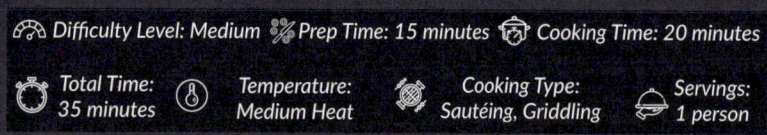

- Difficulty Level: Medium
- Prep Time: 15 minutes
- Cooking Time: 20 minutes
- Total Time: 35 minutes
- Temperature: Medium Heat
- Cooking Type: Sautéing, Griddling
- Servings: 1 person

Ingredients:

- 1/2 cup black beans, drained and rinsed
- 1/2 cup corn kernels
- 1/4 cup diced bell pepper
- 1/4 cup diced onion
- 1/2 cup enchilada sauce
- 2 small corn tortillas
- 1/4 cup shredded cheddar cheese
- 1 tbsp olive oil
- 1 tsp cumin
- Salt and pepper to taste

Instructions:

1. Cook the Veggies: Preheat the griddle to medium heat. Drizzle olive oil and sauté the diced bell pepper and onion until tender. Add black beans, corn, cumin, salt, and pepper. Cook for an additional 2-3 minutes.
2. Assemble the Enchiladas: Fill the tortillas with the black bean and corn mixture. Roll up and place the seam side down on the griddle. Top with enchilada sauce and shredded cheese.
3. Cook the Enchiladas: Cover with a press lid and cook for about 5-7 minutes until the cheese is melted and bubbly.
4. Serve immediately.

Serving Suggestions:
1. Serve with a side of Mexican rice or a fresh green salad.

Nutritional value (per serving):
Calories: 300 | Protein: 12g
Carbohydrates: 40g | Fats: 12g | Fiber: 8g

109. Carne Asada Burritos

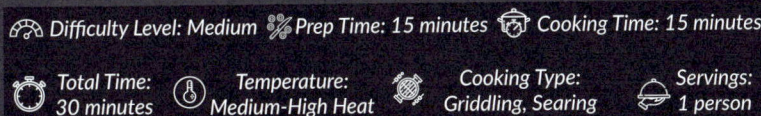

- Difficulty Level: Medium
- Prep Time: 15 minutes
- Cooking Time: 15 minutes
- Total Time: 30 minutes
- Temperature: Medium-High Heat
- Cooking Type: Griddling, Searing
- Servings: 1 person

Ingredients:
- 1/4 lb flank steak, marinated
- 1 large flour tortilla
- 1/4 cup cooked rice
- 1/4 cup black beans, drained and rinsed
- 1/4 cup diced tomatoes
- 1/4 cup shredded lettuce
- 1/4 cup shredded cheese
- 2 tbsp guacamole
- 1 tbsp olive oil
- 1 tbsp lime juice
- Salt and pepper to taste

Instructions:
1. Marinate the Steak: Marinate the flank steak in lime juice, salt, and pepper for at least 30 minutes.
2. Preheat the Griddle: Set your gas griddle to medium-high heat.
3. Cook the Steak: Place the steak on the griddle and cook for about 4-5 minutes per side until desired doneness. Remove and let it rest before slicing.
4. Assemble the Burrito: Place the cooked rice, black beans, diced tomatoes, shredded lettuce, shredded cheese, and sliced steak on the tortilla. Top with guacamole.
5. Roll the Burrito: Roll up the burrito, folding in the sides.
6. Serve immediately.

Serving Suggestions:
1. Serve with a side of salsa or a fresh green salad.

Nutritional value (per serving):
Calories: 500 | Protein: 35g
Carbohydrates: 40g | Fats: 20g | Fiber: 6g

ITALIAN COUSIN RECIPES

110. Margherita Grilled Pizza

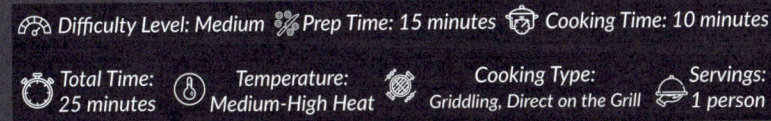

- Difficulty Level: Medium
- Prep Time: 15 minutes
- Cooking Time: 10 minutes
- Total Time: 25 minutes
- Temperature: Medium-High Heat
- Cooking Type: Griddling, Direct on the Grill
- Servings: 1 person

Ingredients:
- 1 small pizza dough ball
- 1/2 cup pizza sauce
- 1/2 cup fresh mozzarella, sliced
- 1/4 cup fresh basil leaves
- 1 tbsp olive oil
- Salt and pepper to taste

Instructions:
1. Preheat the Griddle: Set your gas griddle to medium-high heat.
2. Prepare the Dough: Roll out the pizza dough into a small circle. Brush both sides with olive oil.
3. Cook the Dough: Place the dough on the griddle and cook for about 2-3 minutes per side until lightly browned.
4. Add the Toppings: Spread pizza sauce over the dough, then add slices of fresh mozzarella. Season with salt and pepper.
5. Melt the Cheese: Cover the pizza with a pressed lid and cook for an additional 2-3 minutes until the cheese is melted and bubbly.
6. Finish with Basil: Remove the pizza from the griddle and top with fresh basil leaves.
7. Serve immediately.

Nutritional value (per serving):
Calories: 400 | Protein: 15g
Carbohydrates: 50g | Fats: 15g | Fiber: 4g

Serving Suggestions:
1. Serve with a side of mixed greens or a simple Caesar salad.

111. Garlic Shrimp Scampi

Difficulty Level: Easy Prep Time: 10 minutes Cooking Time: 10 minutes
Total Time: 20 minutes Temperature: Medium-High Heat Cooking Type: Searing, Sautéing Servings: 1 person

Ingredients:

- 8 large shrimp, peeled and deveined
- 1/2 cup sliced bell peppers (red, yellow, green)
- 1/4 cup sliced onion
- 2 tbsp olive oil
- 1 tsp fajita seasoning
- Salt and pepper to taste
- 2 small flour tortillas

Nutritional value (per serving):
Calories: 300 | Protein: 25g
Carbohydrates: 5g | Fats: 18g
Fiber: 1g

Instructions:

1. Preheat the Griddle: Set your gas griddle to medium-high heat.
2. Cook the Shrimp: Drizzle olive oil on the griddle. Add the shrimp and cook for about 2-3 minutes per side until pink and opaque. Remove from the griddle and set aside.
3. Make the Sauce: Add butter and minced garlic to the griddle. Cook until the garlic is fragrant, about 1 minute. Stir in lemon juice, salt, and pepper.
4. Combine and Serve: Return the shrimp to the griddle and toss to coat with the sauce. Sprinkle with chopped parsley.
5. Serve immediately.

Serving Suggestions:
1. Serve with a side of pasta or a fresh salad.

112. Pesto Chicken Panini

Difficulty Level: Easy Prep Time: 10 minutes Cooking Time: 10 minutes
Total Time: 20 minutes Temperature: Medium-High Heat Cooking Type: Griddling, Searing Servings: 1 person

Ingredients:

- 1 boneless, skinless chicken breast
- 2 slices ciabatta bread
- 2 tbsp pesto
- 1/4 cup sliced mozzarella cheese
- 1/4 cup roasted red peppers
- 1 tbsp olive oil
- Salt and pepper to taste

Nutritional value (per serving):
Calories: 400 | Protein: 30g
Carbohydrates: 30g | Fats: 18g | Fiber: 2g

Instructions:

1. Preheat the Griddle: Set your gas griddle to medium heat.
2. Cook the Chicken: Drizzle olive oil on the griddle. Season the chicken breast with salt and pepper and cook for about 5-6 minutes per side until the internal temperature reaches 165°F (74°C). Remove and slice.
3. Assemble the Panini: Spread pesto on one side of each slice of ciabatta bread. Layer sliced chicken, mozzarella cheese, and roasted red peppers between the bread slices.
4. Cook the Panini: Place the panini on the griddle and press down with a press lid. Cook for about 3-4 minutes per side until the bread is golden brown and the cheese is melted.
5. Serve immediately.

Serving Suggestions:
1. Serve with a side of mixed greens or tomato soup.

113. Caprese Salad with Balsamic Glaze

- Difficulty Level: Easy
- Prep Time: 10 minutes
- Cooking Time: 0 minutes
- Total Time: 10 minutes
- Servings: 1 person

Ingredients:
- 1 large tomato, sliced
- 1/4 cup fresh mozzarella, sliced
- 1/4 cup fresh basil leaves
- 1 tbsp olive oil
- 1 tbsp balsamic glaze
- Salt and pepper to taste

Instructions:
1. Assemble the Salad: Arrange slices of tomato and mozzarella on a plate, alternating them. Tuck fresh basil leaves between the slices.
2. Dress the Salad: Drizzle olive oil and balsamic glaze over the salad. Season with salt and pepper.
3. Serve immediately.

Serving Suggestions:
1. Serve as an appetizer or side dish with grilled meats.

Nutritional value (per serving):
Calories: 200 | Protein: 10g
Carbohydrates: 8g | Fats: 15g
Fiber: 2g

114. Sausage and Pepper Hoagies

- Difficulty Level: Medium
- Prep Time: 10 minutes
- Cooking Time: 15 minutes
- Total Time: 25 minutes
- Temperature: Medium-High Heat
- Cooking Type: Griddling, Searing
- Servings: 1 person

Ingredients:
- 1 Italian sausage link
- 1/2 cup sliced bell peppers
- 1/4 cup sliced onions
- 1 hoagie roll
- 1 tbsp olive oil
- 1/4 cup marinara sauce
- 1/4 cup shredded mozzarella cheese
- Salt and pepper to taste

Instructions:
1. Preheat the Griddle: Set your gas griddle to medium-high heat.
Cook the Sausage: Place the sausage on the griddle and cook for about 10 minutes, turning occasionally, until cooked through. Remove and slice.
Cook the Peppers and Onions: Drizzle olive oil on the griddle. Add bell peppers and onions, cooking until tender and slightly charred, about 5-7 minutes. Season with salt and pepper.
Assemble the Hoagie: Toast the Hoagie roll on the griddle for 1-2 minutes until golden. Layer the sliced sausage, peppers, onions, marinara sauce, and shredded mozzarella cheese in the hoagie roll.
Serve immediately.

Serving Suggestions:
1. Serve with a side of chips or a simple salad.

Nutritional value (per serving):
Calories: 450 | Protein: 20g
Carbohydrates: 40g | Fats: 22g | Fiber: 4g

115. Grilled Vegetable Antipasto

Difficulty Level: Easy | Prep Time: 15 minutes | Cooking Time: 15 minutes
Total Time: 30 minutes | Temperature: Medium-High Heat | Cooking Type: Griddling, Searing | Servings: 1 person

Ingredients:
- 1 small zucchini, sliced
- 1 small eggplant, sliced
- 1 red bell pepper, cut into strips
- 1 yellow bell pepper, cut into strips
- 1/2 red onion, sliced
- 2 tbsp olive oil
- 1 tbsp balsamic vinegar
- 1 tsp dried oregano
- Salt and pepper to taste
- Fresh basil leaves for garnish

Instructions:
1. Preheat the Griddle: Set your gas griddle to medium-high heat.
2. Prepare the Vegetables: In a large bowl, toss the sliced zucchini, eggplant, bell peppers, and red onion with olive oil, balsamic vinegar, dried oregano, salt, and pepper.
3. Cook the Vegetables: Place the vegetables on the griddle. Cook for about 5-7 minutes per side until tender and slightly charred.
4. Serve: Arrange the grilled vegetables on a plate and garnish with fresh basil leaves.

Serving Suggestions:
1. Serve with a side of crusty bread and a drizzle of extra balsamic vinegar or olive oil.

Nutritional value (per serving):
Calories: 200 | Protein: 4g
Carbohydrates: 20g | Fats: 12g | Fiber: 6g

116. Lemon Herb Grilled Chicken Piccata

Difficulty Level: Medium | Prep Time: 10 minutes | Cooking Time: 15 minutes
Total Time: 25 minutes | Temperature: Medium-High Heat | Cooking Type: Griddling, Searing, Sautéing | Servings: 1 person

Ingredients:
- 1 boneless, skinless chicken breast
- 2 tbsp olive oil
- 2 tbsp lemon juice
- 1 tsp lemon zest
- 1 tbsp capers, drained
- 1 garlic clove, minced
- 1 tbsp chopped fresh parsley
- 1 tbsp butter
- Salt and pepper to taste

Instructions:
1. Preheat the Griddle: Set your gas griddle to medium-high heat.
2. Prepare the Chicken: Season the chicken breast with salt and pepper. In a small bowl, mix olive oil, lemon juice, lemon zest, and minced garlic. Marinate the chicken breast in this mixture for at least 10 minutes.
3. Cook the Chicken: Place the chicken breast on the griddle and cook for about 5-6 minutes per side until the internal temperature reaches 165°F (74°C). Remove and let it rest.
4. Prepare the Sauce: In a small saucepan on the griddle, melt butter. Add capers and chopped parsley, stirring for about 1-2 minutes until fragrant.
5. Serve: Slice the chicken and drizzle with the caper-butter sauce. Garnish with additional lemon zest and parsley.

Serving Suggestions:
1. Serve with a side of sautéed spinach or a light pasta dish.

Nutritional value (per serving):
Calories: 350 | Protein: 30g
Carbohydrates: 10g | Fats: 20g | Fiber: 2g

ASIAN CUISINE RECIPES

117. Ginger Soy Chicken Stir-Fry

Difficulty Level: Easy | Prep Time: 15 minutes | Cooking Time: 10 minutes
Total Time: 25 minutes | Temperature: Medium-High Heat | Cooking Type: Sautéing, Griddling | Servings: 1 person

Ingredients:
- 1 boneless, skinless chicken breast, thinly sliced
- 1 tbsp soy sauce
- 1 tbsp oyster sauce
- 1 tbsp olive oil
- 1 tbsp grated fresh ginger
- 2 garlic cloves, minced
- 1/2 cup sliced bell pepper
- 1/2 cup broccoli florets
- 1/4 cup sliced carrots
- 1/4 cup sliced green onions
- Salt and pepper to taste
- Cooked rice for serving

Instructions:
1. Preheat the Griddle: Set your gas griddle to medium-high heat.
2. Prepare the Chicken: In a bowl, mix soy sauce, oyster sauce, grated ginger, and minced garlic. Add the sliced chicken and marinate for 10 minutes.
3. Cook the Chicken: Drizzle olive oil on the griddle. Add the chicken and cook for about 5 minutes until browned and cooked through. Remove and set aside.
4. Cook the Vegetables: Add the bell pepper, broccoli, carrots, and green onions to the griddle. Cook for about 4-5 minutes until tender.
5. Combine and Serve: Return the chicken to the griddle, toss to combine with the vegetables, and cook for an additional 1-2 minutes. Serve over cooked rice.

Serving Suggestions:
1. Garnish with sesame seeds and serve with a side of steamed rice.

Nutritional value (per serving):
Calories: 300 | Protein: 25g | Carbohydrates: 15g | Fats: 12g | Fiber: 2g

118. Beef and Broccoli Stir-Fry

Difficulty Level: Easy | Prep Time: 10 minutes | Cooking Time: 10 minutes
Total Time: 20 minutes | Temperature: Medium-High Heat | Cooking Type: Sautéing, Griddling | Servings: 1 person

Ingredients:
- 1/4 lb beef sirloin, thinly sliced
- 1 tbsp soy sauce
- 1 tbsp hoisin sauce
- 1 tbsp olive oil
- 1 garlic clove, minced
- 1/2 cup broccoli florets
- 1/4 cup sliced onions
- 1/4 cup sliced bell pepper
- Salt and pepper to taste
- Cooked rice for serving

Instructions:
1. Preheat the Griddle: Set your gas griddle to medium-high heat.
2. Prepare the Beef: In a bowl, mix soy sauce, hoisin sauce, and minced garlic. Add the sliced beef and marinate for 10 minutes.
3. Cook the Beef: Drizzle olive oil on the griddle. Add the beef and cook for about 3-4 minutes until browned. Remove and set aside.
4. Cook the Vegetables: Add the broccoli, onions, and bell pepper to the griddle. Cook for about 5 minutes until tender.
5. Combine and Serve: Return the beef to the griddle, toss to combine with the vegetables, and cook for an additional 1-2 minutes. Serve over cooked rice.

Serving Suggestions:
1. Garnish with chopped green onions and sesame seeds.

Nutritional value (per serving):
Calories: 350 | Protein: 30g | Carbohydrates: 15g | Fats: 18g | Fiber: 3g

119. Spicy Szechuan Shrimp

- Difficulty Level: Medium
- Prep Time: 10 minutes
- Cooking Time: 10 minutes
- Total Time: 20 minutes
- Temperature: Medium-High Heat
- Cooking Type: Sautéing, Griddling
- Servings: 1 person

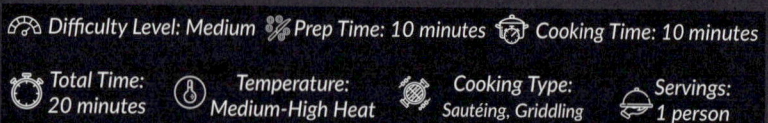

Ingredients:
- 8 large shrimp, peeled and deveined
- 1 tbsp soy sauce
- 1 tbsp Szechuan chili paste
- 1 tbsp olive oil
- 1 garlic clove, minced
- 1/4 cup sliced bell pepper
- 1/4 cup sliced onions
- 1/4 cup snap peas
- Salt and pepper to taste
- Cooked rice for serving

Instructions:
1. Preheat the Griddle: Set your gas griddle to medium-high heat.
2. Prepare the Shrimp: In a bowl, mix soy sauce, Szechuan chili paste, and minced garlic. Add the shrimp and marinate for 5 minutes.
3. Cook the Shrimp: Drizzle olive oil on the griddle. Add the shrimp and cook for about 2-3 minutes per side until pink and opaque. Remove and set aside.
4. Cook the Vegetables: Add the bell pepper, onions, and snap peas to the griddle. Cook for about 4-5 minutes until tender.
5. Combine and Serve: Return the shrimp to the griddle, toss to combine with the vegetables, and cook for an additional 1-2 minutes. Serve over cooked rice.

Nutritional value (per serving):
Calories: 250 | Protein: 25g | Carbohydrates: 10g | Fats: 12g | Fiber: 2g

Serving Suggestions:
1. Garnish with chopped green onions and a squeeze of lime juice.

120. Teriyaki Chicken Bowls with Steamed Rice

- Difficulty Level: Easy
- Prep Time: 15 minutes
- Cooking Time: 15 minutes
- Total Time: 30 minutes
- Temperature: Medium-High Heat
- Cooking Type: Sautéing, Griddling
- Servings: 1 person

Ingredients:
- 1 boneless, skinless chicken breast, cubed
- 2 tbsp teriyaki sauce
- 1 tbsp olive oil
- 1 garlic clove, minced
- 1/2 cup broccoli florets
- 1/4 cup sliced bell pepper
- 1/4 cup sliced carrots
- Salt and pepper to taste
- Cooked rice for serving

Instructions:
1. Marinate the Chicken: In a bowl, mix teriyaki sauce and minced garlic. Add the cubed chicken and marinate for at least 30 minutes.
2. Preheat the Griddle: Set your gas griddle to medium-high heat.
3. Cook the Chicken: Drizzle olive oil on the griddle. Add the chicken and cook for about 5-7 minutes until browned and cooked through. Remove and set aside.
4. Cook the Vegetables: Add the broccoli, bell pepper, and carrots to the griddle. Cook for about 5 minutes until tender.
5. Combine and Serve: Return the chicken to the griddle, toss to combine with the vegetables, and cook for an additional 1-2 minutes. Serve over cooked rice.

Nutritional value (per serving):
Calories: 400 | Protein: 30g | Carbohydrates: 45g | Fats: 12g | Fiber: 4g

Serving Suggestions:
1. Garnish with sesame seeds and chopped green onions.

121. Soy Glazed Salmon with Sesame

Difficulty Level: Medium | Prep Time: 10 minutes | Cooking Time: 10 minutes
Total Time: 20 minutes | Temperature: Medium-High Heat | Cooking Type: Searing, Griddling | Servings: 1 person

Ingredients:
- 6 oz salmon fillet
- 2 tbsp soy sauce
- 1 tbsp honey
- 1 tbsp olive oil
- 1 tsp sesame oil
- 1 garlic clove, minced
- 1 tsp grated fresh ginger
- 1 tbsp sesame seeds
- 1 green onion, sliced

Instructions:
1. Marinate the Salmon: In a bowl, mix soy sauce, honey, sesame oil, minced garlic, and grated ginger. Marinate the salmon fillet in the mixture for at least 10 minutes.
2. Preheat the Griddle: Set your gas griddle to medium-high heat.
3. Cook the Salmon: Drizzle olive oil on the griddle. Place the salmon fillet skin side down on the griddle and cook for about 4-5 minutes. Flip the salmon and cook for an additional 3-4 minutes until cooked through.
4. Serve: Sprinkle sesame seeds and sliced green onion over the salmon and serve immediately.

Serving Suggestions:
1. Serve with a side of steamed rice or sautéed vegetables.

Nutritional value (per serving):
Calories: 350 | Protein: 30g | Carbohydrates: 10g | Fats: 20g | Fiber: 1g

122. Sweet and Sour Pork Stir-Fry

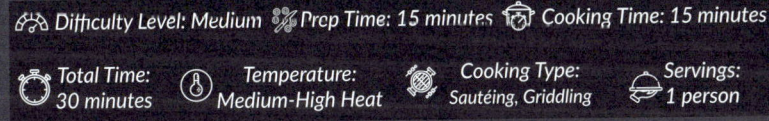

Difficulty Level: Medium | Prep Time: 15 minutes | Cooking Time: 15 minutes
Total Time: 30 minutes | Temperature: Medium-High Heat | Cooking Type: Sautéing, Griddling | Servings: 1 person

Ingredients:
- 1/4 lb pork tenderloin, thinly sliced
- 1/2 cup diced pineapple
- 1/4 cup diced bell pepper
- 1/4 cup diced onions
- 2 tbsp sweet and sour sauce
- 1 tbsp olive oil
- 1 garlic clove, minced
- Salt and pepper to taste
- Cooked rice for serving

Instructions:
1. Preheat the Griddle: Set your gas griddle to medium-high heat.
2. Prepare the Pork: Season the sliced pork with salt and pepper.
3. Cook the Pork: Drizzle olive oil on the griddle. Add the pork and cook for about 5 minutes until browned and cooked through. Remove and set aside.
4. Cook the Vegetables: Add the pineapple, bell pepper, and onions to the griddle. Cook for about 5 minutes until tender.
5. Combine and Serve: Return the pork to the griddle, toss to combine with the vegetables, and add sweet and sour sauce. Cook for an additional 1-2 minutes. Serve over cooked rice.

Serving Suggestions:
1. Garnish with chopped green onions and serve with a side of steamed vegetables.

Nutritional value (per serving):
Calories: 400 | Protein: 25g | Carbohydrates: 30g | Fats: 18g | Fiber: 3g

LATIN-AMERICAN RECIPES

123. Argentinian Grilled Chimichurri Steak

- Difficulty Level: Medium
- Prep Time: 15 minutes
- Cooking Time: 10 minutes
- Total Time: 25 minutes
- Temperature: Medium-High Heat
- Cooking Type: Searing, Griddling
- Servings: 1 person

Ingredients:

For the Steak:
- 8 oz flank steak
- 1 tbsp olive oil
- Salt and pepper to taste

For the Chimichurri Sauce:
- 1/4 cup fresh parsley, chopped
- 1/4 cup fresh cilantro, chopped
- 2 garlic cloves, minced
- 1 tbsp red wine vinegar
- 1/4 cup olive oil
- 1/2 tsp red pepper flakes
- Salt and pepper to taste

Instructions:

1. Preheat the Griddle: Set your gas griddle to medium-high heat.
2. Prepare the Chimichurri Sauce: In a bowl, mix parsley, cilantro, minced garlic, red wine vinegar, olive oil, red pepper flakes, salt, and pepper. Set aside.
3. Season the Steak: Drizzle olive oil over the steak and season with salt and pepper.
4. Cook the Steak: Place the steak on the griddle and cook for about 4-5 minutes per side until desired doneness. Remove and let it rest for 5 minutes.
5. Serve: Slice the steak against the grain and top with chimichurri sauce.

Serving Suggestions:
1. Serve with a side of grilled vegetables or a fresh salad.

Nutritional value (per serving):

Calories: 400 | Protein: 35g
Carbohydrates: 4g | Fats: 26g
Fiber: 1g

124. Peruvian Chicken with Aji Verde Sauce

- Difficulty Level: Medium
- Prep Time: 20 minutes
- Cooking Time: 15 minutes
- Total Time: 35 minutes
- Temperature: Medium-High Heat
- Cooking Type: Searing, Griddling
- Servings: 1 person

Ingredients:

For the Chicken:
- 1 boneless, skinless chicken breast
- 2 tbsp olive oil
- 1 tbsp lime juice
- 1 garlic clove, minced
- 1 tsp cumin
- 1 tsp paprika
- Salt and pepper to taste

For the Aji Verde Sauce:
- 1/4 cup mayonnaise
- 1/4 cup Greek yogurt
- 1 tbsp aji amarillo paste (or substitute with a small jalapeño, seeded)
- 1 garlic clove
- 1/4 cup fresh cilantro
- 1 tbsp lime juice
- Salt and pepper to taste

Instructions:

1. Marinate the Chicken: In a bowl, mix olive oil, lime juice, minced garlic, cumin, paprika, salt, and pepper. Marinate the chicken breast in the mixture for at least 30 minutes.
2. Prepare the Aji Verde Sauce: In a blender, combine mayonnaise, Greek yogurt, aji amarillo paste, garlic, cilantro, lime juice, salt, and pepper. Blend until smooth and set aside.
3. Preheat the Griddle: Set your gas griddle to medium-high heat.
4. Cook the Chicken: Place the chicken breast on the griddle and cook for about 5-7 minutes per side until the internal temperature reaches 165°F (74°C). Remove and let it rest for 5 minutes.
5. Serve: Slice the chicken and serve with aji verde sauce.

Serving Suggestions:
1. Serve with a side of quinoa or roasted potatoes.

Nutritional value (per serving):

Calories: 350 | Protein: 30g
Carbohydrates: 10g | Fats: 22g | Fiber: 2g

125. Cuban Mojo Pork Tacos
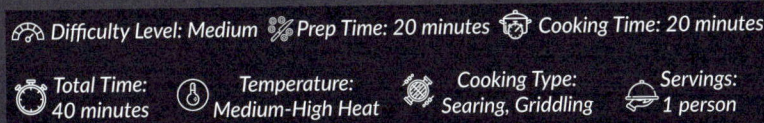

- Difficulty Level: Medium
- Prep Time: 20 minutes
- Cooking Time: 20 minutes
- Total Time: 40 minutes
- Temperature: Medium-High Heat
- Cooking Type: Searing, Griddling
- Servings: 1 person

Ingredients:

For the Pork:
- 1/2 lb pork shoulder, thinly sliced
- 2 tbsp olive oil
- 1 tbsp orange juice
- 1 tbsp lime juice
- 2 garlic cloves, minced
- 1 tsp cumin
- Salt and pepper to taste

For the Tacos:
- 2 small corn tortillas
- 1/4 cup shredded lettuce
- 1/4 cup diced tomatoes
- 1/4 cup sliced red onion
- Fresh cilantro leaves for garnish

Instructions:
1. Marinate the Pork: In a bowl, mix olive oil, orange juice, lime juice, minced garlic, cumin, salt, and pepper. Marinate the sliced pork in the mixture for at least 30 minutes.
2. Preheat the Griddle: Set your gas griddle to medium-high heat.
3. Cook the Pork: Place the pork on the griddle and cook for about 8-10 minutes until cooked through and slightly crispy.
4. Warm the Tortillas: Place the tortillas on the griddle for about 1 minute per side until warm.
5. Assemble the Tacos: Fill the tortillas with cooked pork, shredded lettuce, diced tomatoes, and sliced red onion. Garnish with fresh cilantro leaves.
6. Serve immediately.

Serving Suggestions:
1. Serve with a side of black beans or rice.

Nutritional value (per serving):
Calories: 400 | Protein: 30g
Carbohydrates: 30g | Fats: 18g | Fiber: 4g

126. Chilean Pebre Sauce with Grilled Bread
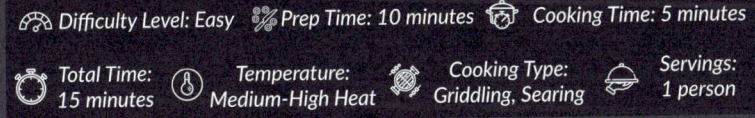

- Difficulty Level: Easy
- Prep Time: 10 minutes
- Cooking Time: 5 minutes
- Total Time: 15 minutes
- Temperature: Medium-High Heat
- Cooking Type: Griddling, Searing
- Servings: 1 person

Ingredients:

For the Pebre Sauce:
- 1/2 cup diced tomatoes
- 1/4 cup diced onions
- 1/4 cup chopped fresh cilantro
- 1 garlic clove, minced
- 1 tbsp red wine vinegar
- 2 tbsp olive oil
- Salt and pepper to taste

For the Grilled Bread:
- 2 slices rustic bread
- 1 tbsp olive oil

Instructions:
1. Prepare the Pebre Sauce: In a bowl, mix diced tomatoes, diced onions, chopped cilantro, minced garlic, red wine vinegar, olive oil, salt, and pepper. Set aside.
2. Preheat the Griddle: Set your gas griddle to medium-high heat.
3. Grill the Bread: Brush the bread slices with olive oil and place them on the griddle. Cook for about 2-3 minutes per side until golden and crispy.
4. Serve the pebre sauce with the grilled bread slices.

Serving Suggestions:
1. Serve as an appetizer or alongside grilled meats.

Nutritional value (per serving):
Calories: 250 | Protein: 6g
Carbohydrates: 40g | Fats: 8g
Fiber: 4g

127. Brazilian Grilled Pineapple with Cinnamon

- Difficulty Level: Easy
- Prep Time: 10 minutes
- Cooking Time: 10 minutes
- Total Time: 20 minutes
- Temperature: Medium-High Heat
- Cooking Type: Griddling, Searing
- Servings: 1 person

Ingredients:
- 4 slices fresh pineapple, cored
- 1 tbsp honey
- 1 tsp ground cinnamon

Nutritional value (per serving):
Calories: 150 | Protein: 1g
Carbohydrates: 38g | Fats: 0g
Fiber: 4g

Instructions:
1. Preheat the Griddle: Set your gas griddle to medium-high heat.
2. Prepare the Pineapple: Brush the pineapple slices with honey and sprinkle with ground cinnamon.
3. Cook the Pineapple: Place the pineapple slices on the griddle and cook for about 3-4 minutes per side until caramelized and golden brown.
4. Serve immediately.

Serving Suggestions:
1. Serve with a scoop of vanilla ice cream or a dollop of whipped cream.

DESSERTS

128. Grilled Peaches with Honey and Mascarpone

- Difficulty Level: Easy
- Prep Time: 5 minutes
- Cooking Time: 10 minutes
- Total Time: 15 minutes
- Temperature: Medium Heat
- Cooking Type: Griddling, Searing
- Servings: 1 person

Ingredients:

For the Peaches:
- 1 ripe peach, halved and pitted
- 1 tbsp olive oil
- 1 tbsp honey

For the Mascarpone Topping:
- 1/4 cup mascarpone cheese
- 1 tbsp honey
- 1/4 tsp vanilla extract

For Garnish:
- Fresh mint leaves
- Crushed nuts (optional)

Nutritional value (per serving):
Calories: 250 | Protein: 4g
Carbohydrates: 38g | Fats: 12g | Fiber: 3g

Instructions:
1. Preheat the Griddle
   - Set your gas griddle to medium heat.
2. Prepare the Peaches
   - Brush the Peach Halves: Lightly brush the cut sides of the peach halves with olive oil to prevent sticking and promote even caramelization.
   - Drizzle with Honey: Drizzle 1 tbsp of honey over the cut sides of the peaches.
3. Grill the Peaches
   - Place on Griddle: Place the peach halves, cut side down, on the griddle.
   - Cook: Grill for about 4-5 minutes until the peaches are caramelized and have grill marks.
   - Flip: Flip the peaches and grill for an additional 3-4 minutes until the peaches are tender.
4. Prepare the Mascarpone Topping
   - Mix Ingredients: In a small bowl, combine the mascarpone cheese, 1 tbsp honey, and 1/4 tsp vanilla extract. Mix until smooth and creamy.
5. Assemble and Serve
   - Plate the Peaches: Place the grilled peach halves on a serving plate, cut side up.
   - Add Topping: Spoon a generous dollop of the mascarpone mixture onto each peach half.
   - Drizzle with Honey: Drizzle the remaining honey over the peaches.
   - Garnish: Garnish with fresh mint leaves and crushed nuts, if using.

129. Cinnamon Sugar Grilled Pineapple Rings

- Difficulty Level: Easy
- Prep Time: 5 minutes
- Cooking Time: 10 minutes
- Total Time: 15 minutes
- Temperature: Medium-High Heat
- Cooking Type: Griddling, Searing
- Servings: 1 person

Ingredients:
- 4 pineapple rings
- 1 tbsp melted butter
- 1 tbsp brown sugar
- 1/2 tsp ground cinnamon

Nutritional value (per serving):
Calories: 150 | Protein: 1g
Carbohydrates: 38g | Fats: 1g
Fiber: 4g

Instructions:
1. Preheat the Griddle: Set your gas griddle to medium-high heat.
2. Prepare the Pineapple: Brush the pineapple rings with melted butter. In a small bowl, mix brown sugar and ground cinnamon. Sprinkle the mixture over both sides of the pineapple rings.
3. Grill the Pineapple: Place the pineapple rings on the griddle and cook for about 3-4 minutes per side until caramelized and golden brown.
4. Serve immediately.

Serving Suggestions:
1. Serve with a scoop of coconut ice cream or a drizzle of caramel sauce.

130. Griddled Pound Cake with Berries and Cream

- Difficulty Level: Easy
- Prep Time: 5 minutes
- Cooking Time: 5 minutes
- Total Time: 10 minutes
- Temperature: Medium Heat
- Cooking Type: Griddling, Searing
- Servings: 1 person

Ingredients:
- 2 slices of pound cake
- 1/4 cup mixed berries (strawberries, blueberries, raspberries)
- 1 tbsp butter
- Whipped cream for serving

Nutritional value (per serving):
Calories: 300 | Protein: 4g
Carbohydrates: 40g | Fats: 15g | Fiber: 2g

Instructions:
1. Preheat the Griddle: Set your gas griddle to medium heat.
2. Prepare the Pound Cake: Butter both sides of the pound cake slices.
3. Grill the Pound Cake: Place the pound cake slices on the griddle and cook for about 2-3 minutes per side until golden brown.
4. Serve: Top the grilled pound cake with mixed berries and a dollop of whipped cream.

Serving Suggestions:
1. Serve with a drizzle of berry sauce or a sprinkle of powdered sugar.

131. S'mores Quesadillas

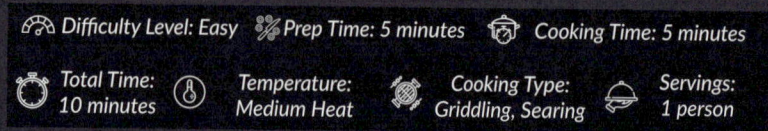

Difficulty Level: Easy | Prep Time: 5 minutes | Cooking Time: 5 minutes
Total Time: 10 minutes | Temperature: Medium Heat | Cooking Type: Griddling, Searing | Servings: 1 person

Ingredients:
- 1 large flour tortilla
- 1/4 cup mini marshmallows
- 1/4 cup chocolate chips
- 2 graham crackers, crushed

Nutritional value (per serving):
Calories: 350 | Protein: 5g | Carbohydrates: 55g | Fats: 15g | Fiber: 3g

Instructions:
1. Preheat the Griddle: Set your gas griddle to medium heat.
2. Assemble the Quesadilla: Sprinkle half of the tortilla with mini marshmallows, chocolate chips, and crushed graham crackers. Fold the tortilla in half to enclose the filling.
3. Grill the Quesadilla: Place the quesadilla on the griddle and cook for about 2-3 minutes per side until golden brown and the filling is melted.
4. Serve: Cut into wedges and serve immediately.

Serving Suggestions:
1. Serve with a drizzle of chocolate sauce or a side of vanilla ice cream.

SNACKS

132. Grilled Cheese Sandwiches with Tomato Soup Dip

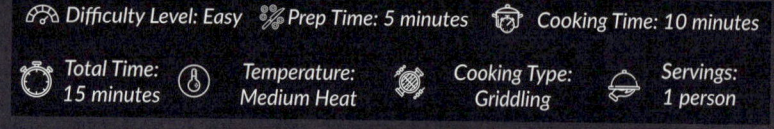

Difficulty Level: Easy | Prep Time: 5 minutes | Cooking Time: 10 minutes
Total Time: 15 minutes | Temperature: Medium Heat | Cooking Type: Griddling | Servings: 1 person

Ingredients:
For the Grilled Cheese:
- 2 slices of bread
- 1/4 cup shredded cheddar cheese
- 1/4 cup shredded mozzarella cheese
- 1 tbsp butter

For the Tomato Soup Dip:
- 1/2 cup tomato soup (canned or homemade)
- 1 tbsp heavy cream (optional)
- Salt and pepper to taste

Nutritional value (per serving):
Calories: 350 | Protein: 12g | Carbohydrates: 30g | Fats: 20g | Fiber: 3g

Instructions:
1. Preheat the Griddle: Set your gas griddle to medium heat.
2. Prepare the Sandwich: Butter one side of each bread slice. Place one slice, butter side down, on the griddle. Top with shredded cheddar and mozzarella cheese. Place the second slice of bread on top, butter side up.
3. Cook the Sandwich: Cook for about 3-4 minutes per side until the bread is golden brown and the cheese is melted.
4. Prepare the Tomato Soup Dip: While the sandwich is cooking, heat the tomato soup in a small saucepan on the griddle. Stir in heavy cream, if using, and season with salt and pepper.
5. Serve: Cut the grilled cheese sandwich into strips and serve with the tomato soup dip.

Serving Suggestions:
1. Serve with a side of pickles or a small green salad.

133. Crispy Zucchini Fritters

Difficulty Level: Medium | *Prep Time:* 10 minutes | *Cooking Time:* 15 minutes
Total Time: 25 minutes | *Temperature:* Medium-High Heat | *Cooking Type:* Searing, Griddling | *Servings:* 1 person

Ingredients:
- 1 medium zucchini, grated
- 1/4 cup grated Parmesan cheese
- 1/4 cup flour
- 1 egg, beaten
- 1 garlic clove, minced
- 1 tbsp chopped fresh parsley
- Salt and pepper to taste
- 2 tbsp olive oil

Instructions:
1. Preheat the Griddle: Set your gas griddle to medium-high heat.
2. Prepare the Zucchini: Place the grated zucchini in a clean kitchen towel and squeeze out as much liquid as possible.
3. Make the Batter: In a bowl, combine the grated zucchini, Parmesan cheese, flour, beaten egg, minced garlic, chopped parsley, salt, and pepper. Mix well.
4. Cook the Fritters: Drizzle olive oil on the griddle. Drop spoonfuls of the batter onto the griddle and flatten them slightly. Cook for about 3-4 minutes per side until golden brown and crispy.
5. Serve immediately.

Serving Suggestions:
1. Serve with a side of sour cream or a light yogurt dip.

Nutritional value (per serving):
Calories: 200 | Protein: 6g
Carbohydrates: 20g | Fats: 10g | Fiber: 3g

134. Loaded Nachos with Griddled Beef

Difficulty Level: Medium | *Prep Time:* 10 minutes | *Cooking Time:* 15 minutes
Total Time: 25 minutes | *Temperature:* Medium-High Heat | *Cooking Type:* Searing, Griddling | *Servings:* 1 person

Ingredients:
For the Beef:
- 1/4 lb ground beef
- 1 tbsp taco seasoning
- 1 tbsp olive oil
- Salt and pepper to taste

For the Nachos:
- 1 cup tortilla chips
- 1/2 cup shredded cheddar cheese
- 1/4 cup shredded Monterey Jack cheese
- 1/4 cup diced tomatoes
- 1/4 cup sliced jalapeños
- 1/4 cup sliced black olives
- 1/4 cup sour cream
- 2 tbsp chopped fresh cilantro

Instructions:
1. Preheat the Griddle: Set your gas griddle to medium-high heat.
2. Cook the Beef: Drizzle olive oil on the griddle. Add the ground beef and cook, breaking it up with a spatula, until browned. Stir in taco seasoning and cook for an additional 2 minutes. Remove and set aside.
3. Assemble the Nachos: Spread the tortilla chips on a large plate. Layer with cooked beef, shredded cheddar and Monterey Jack cheese, diced tomatoes, sliced jalapeños, and sliced black olives.
4. Melt the Cheese: Place the plate on the griddle (using an oven-safe plate or a heatproof griddle-safe plate) and cook for about 3-5 minutes until the cheese is melted.
5. Serve: Top with sour cream and chopped fresh cilantro.

Serving Suggestions:
1. Serve with a side of guacamole or salsa.

Nutritional value (per serving):
Calories: 500 | Protein: 25g
Carbohydrates: 50g | Fats: 25g | Fiber: 5g

135. Cheesy Queso Dip with Griddled Jalapeños

Difficulty Level: Easy	Prep Time: 5 minutes	Cooking Time: 10 minutes
Total Time: 15 minutes	Temperature: Medium Heat	Cooking Type: Searing, Griddling	Servings: 1 person

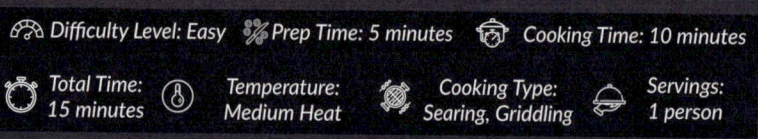

Ingredients:
- 1 cup shredded cheddar cheese
- 1 cup shredded Monterey Jack cheese
- 1/2 cup milk
- 1 tbsp butter
- 1 garlic clove, minced
- 2 jalapeños, sliced
- Salt and pepper to taste
- Tortilla chips for serving

Nutritional value *(per serving)*:
Calories: 300 | Protein: 12g
Carbohydrates: 15g | Fats: 20g | Fiber: 2g

Instructions:
1. **Preheat the Griddle:** Set your gas griddle to medium heat.
2. **Cook the Jalapeños:** Place the sliced jalapeños on the griddle and cook for about 2-3 minutes per side until slightly charred. Remove and set aside.
3. **Make the Queso Dip:** In a small saucepan on the griddle, melt butter and add minced garlic. Cook for about 1 minute until fragrant. Add milk and bring to a simmer. Gradually stir in shredded cheddar and Monterey Jack cheese until melted and smooth. Season with salt and pepper.
4. **Serve:** Pour the queso dip into a bowl and top with griddled jalapeños. Serve immediately with tortilla chips.

Serving Suggestions:
1. Serve with a side of salsa or guacamole.

136. Sweet Potato Fries with Spicy Aioli

Difficulty Level: Medium	Prep Time: 10 minutes	Cooking Time: 15 minutes
Total Time: 25 minutes	Temperature: Medium-High Heat	Cooking Type: Searing, Griddling	Servings: 1 person

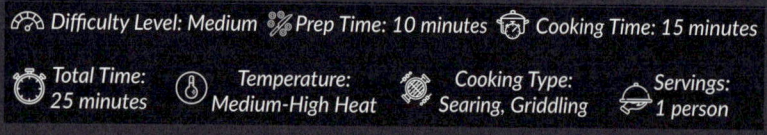

Ingredients:
For the Fries:
- 1 medium sweet potato, cut into fries
- 2 tbsp olive oil
- 1 tsp paprika
- 1/2 tsp garlic powder
- Salt and pepper to taste

For the Spicy Aioli:
- 1/4 cup mayonnaise
- 1 tbsp sriracha sauce
- 1 tsp lime juice
- 1 garlic clove, minced

Instructions:
1. **Preheat the Griddle:** Set your gas griddle to medium-high heat.
2. **Prepare the Fries:** In a bowl, toss the sweet potato fries with olive oil, paprika, garlic powder, salt, and pepper.
3. **Cook the Fries:** Place the sweet potato fries on the griddle and cook for about 10-12 minutes, turning occasionally, until golden brown and crispy.
4. **Make the Aioli:** In a small bowl, mix mayonnaise, sriracha sauce, lime juice, and minced garlic until well combined.
5. Serve the sweet potato fries with spicy aioli.

Serving Suggestions:
1. Serve with a side of ketchup or ranch dressing.

Nutritional value *(per serving)*:
Calories: 250 | Protein: 2g
Carbohydrates: 40g | Fats: 12g | Fiber: 5g

Made in the USA
Thornton, CO
06/08/25 19:13:59

98d34c2b-3138-4823-b6d0-46b7d18d1e58R01